THE TRADITIONAL ENGLISH PUB
A Way of Drinking

THE TRADITIONAL ENGLISH PUB

A Way of Drinking

Ben Davis

THE ARCHITECTURAL PRESS : LONDON

Dedicated to the memory of the Architects Department, Ind Coope Ltd., disbanded on 30 May 1980.

First published in 1981 by The Architectural Press Ltd., London

© Ben Davis 1981

ISBN: 0 85139 055 2

Printed in Great Britain by W & J Mackay Limited, Chatham

CONTENTS

PART IV   DESIGN GUIDE
by Frank Bradbeer

Acknowledgements

I am grateful to my employers, Allied Breweries, for the support they have given in the preparation of this book; for permission to use illustrations, most of which are theirs; and in particular for taking in good part my occasional shafts of wit and asperity at the expense of brewers in general. Without the unstinted encouragement I have received from my boss, Mr R. T. C. Maxwell, the typescript might still be in a scruffy heap on top of the piano at home.

Also I hope that all pub users will share my gratitude to my seniors and colleagues of the 1950's for their priceless contribution to pub design – Carl Fairless, Bill Blair, Jim Witham, Mick Rickard, Vic Howard (deceased), George Salkeld, Roy Woods, Doug Shepherd, John Bellamy, Tony Drew, Stan Schofield and numerous others, all under the beneficent aegis of Mr Neville G. Thompson as Technical Director of Ind Coope and Allsopp Ltd. All I have done is to codify and present the attitudes which evolved from our work together at that time.

Author's Preface

When I had finished writing this book a publisher asked me, "Why do pubs have to be altered?" It is not a bad question. The word 'pub' carries with it associations which are generally agreeable. A homesick dweller in foreign parts may conjure up for himself a picture of his ideal pub. The regular thinks only of his chosen local. Both are indignant at any suggestion of alterations. They like their pubs, imaginary or real, as they are, and perhaps in the past they have suffered the saddening experience of seeing a favourite 'boozer' brought up to date to suit the taste of someone they never met, and whose ideas of a pub differed pretty sharply from theirs.

Alteration work need not be done in such a way as to antagonise and outrage the customers: it can be managed with love, tact and enjoyment, but the fact this is not always achieved is adequately shown by the attitude of suspicion and resentment almost always adopted by the blokes in the bar towards the architect on his first visit to a pub which is to be 'improved'. Years ago the question was, "Are you going to modernise it?" and the inflection on the word 'modernise' left no doubt that it was derogatory. Nowadays they are more likely to ask, "Are you going to lush the place up?" and the same distaste is evident. It is clear that errors must have been made over the years which have left unfavourable impressions in the mind of the pub-going public. Why, they wonder, can you not leave well enough alone?

However, it certainly is not true that all pubs are 'well enough'. The exile's sentimental picture may fit exactly the facts he knows about the pubs he was accustomed to use, but neither he nor the regular is likely to know what shortcomings exist behind the scenes: nor do they know how sadly neglected and uncomfortable are a vast number of pubs which they have never seen. Many have suffered from the sort of alterations they fear for their own, and need restoration. Some have been allowed to fall into a state of squalid clutter and disrepair, and others no longer meet the needs of the people they serve. The pub should not, of course, change its character in response to every fickle breeze of fashion, but it has to cater for a reasonable consensus of demand as far as standards of amenity are concerned. The whole problem herein considered is how it can provide these without at the same time losing its essential character – the qualities which have endeared it to generations of the English and their visitors from overseas in every age. We must be sure in our minds what these are.

The Brewery Trade Director tends to think of the pub as a Retail Outlet; the lawyer sees it as an item of Real Estate, the accountant as a Commercial Asset. The Environmental Health Officer regards it as an amalgam of urinals, drains and bacteria-harbouring surfaces. To the Licensing Magistrate it is merely Premises to which he grants or from which he can withold a Licence. The Fire Officer suspects it is a death-trap. The Excise man knows it is a source of Revenue. The Planning Officer, as often as not, wants to pull it down and make a Public Open Space. The Borough Surveyor fears that it may fall down anyway. All these powerful people are bound to hold attitudes which are, for them, valid, and although they are all heretics in the sense that they choose to present only a part of the truth, each has the duty to insist on his particular requirements. It is hardly surprising, therefore, that the architect, trying to reconcile demands which often conflict with each other, sometimes fails. I hope that in the pages which follow he will find something to encourage him, and to remind him that the customer, because he pays the bills, should be considered first and foremost.

Introduction

The pub is English. The Scots drink in bars, and the Welsh, bless them, will drink anywhere. The splendid Irish had the sense to hold on to the pubs which the English gave them, (and let us be thankful that so many remain unspoiled) but their native manner of drinking is in grocers' shops. As on the Continent, the clear distinction is lacking between drinking-place and non-drinking-place, a distinction which in England is defined by law. In Scotland and Wales where they misunderstood the niceties, the law is (or was until recently) more stringent still. It is therefore in England that we must look for a definition of that mode of social drinking which, at one time unique, is now being copied in many parts of the world.

Attempts overseas to copy the pub can only succeed in so far as the nature of the original is understood and, indeed, it is unlikely that they will be completely successful, because the places are administered under different laws and regulations or under none. However, since it is widely agreed that the English pub at its best can offer a social drinking environment second to none, it is worth making the attempt to analyse and explain the characteristics which are of its essence. This kind of analysis is mistrusted by some because (they say) every pub is an individual and how can one generalise? I answer this by saying that pubs differ no more than people, who despite their vast diversity in form and face, in colour and character, in habits and healthiness, remain recognisable as members of the human race. But if the distinguishing characteristics of people or pubs are missing, the unhappy result is, in either case, a freak or a totally different 'animal'. The things which good pubs, of any period and in all places, have in common are more important than their differences. It is necessary to distinguish between the general and universal on the one hand and the local and ephemeral on the other. No one, I trust, would presume to make *rules*: but the principles which I hope to establish are in the nature of scientific laws which have been discovered. If we ignore them we do so at our peril. As Belloc said, "When you have lost your inns you may drown your empty selves, for you will have lost the heart of England".

1

Let us, however, be strictly unsentimental. As long ago as 1938 *The Architects' Journal* pointed out in a special issue that the essential pub character is important to the brewers who make money out of it. It is equally important to governments, sociologists and social drinkers, and perhaps above all to the licensee, who is the key man in the business. When architects, as many did in the 'Thirties, fail to grasp the pub character, he can do much to retrieve the failure. Conversely, he can quite quickly destroy a great deal of what the architect has created. I, therefore, having offered this acknowledgement of his importance, make no apology for trespassing on his side of the counter. I believe that when anyone building, converting or running a pub departs from certain criteria the result will, to a greater or less degree, fail. I believe that it is possible to arrive at such criteria by defining those qualities which distinguish pubs from other places, and that it is these same qualities which distinguish popular pubs from those which are less successful.

A pub, as we are too often reminded by marketing men, is a retail outlet. If it is nothing more than this it will fail, but the fact cannot be refuted, and in seeking the essentials we must ensure that the mundane physical requirements of delivery, storage and service of the merchandise are also taken care of. Detailed information about those aspects of pub design is given at the end of this book but here my intention is to start where such facts and figures tend to leave off by considering first the social drinker – the all-important customer on whose money the trade depends, and the various relationships which exist between him and the pub he enters. Also, it may be worth noting here that the pub exterior (which will be referred to later) is of secondary importance. This is because, if the customer is disappointed with the inside of an externally attractive pub, he will not stay long, but there are other ways of getting him into a house which doesn't look much from outside. The power of personal recommendation is normally under-valued, but it can overcome a poor exterior, and it is what they find *inside* which keeps people there once they are in, and tempts them to return on future occasions. This is one of the many ways in which pubs differ from shops. It is not in a shopkeeper's interest that customers should linger when they have bought what they want. In a pub, on the other hand, the longer they stay the more they consume.*

The word 'pub' is of course an abbreviation of 'public house'. It is contended by the licensed Trade that this is a misnomer, and that the pub is not really a public place at all. The licensee may exclude anyone without giving a reason. Nevertheless, I think we can say that a pub is a house open to the public at stated times for the purpose of social drinking. Any other purpose, such as eating or entertainment, is incidental. This conveniently narrows the field by excluding licensed restaurants, theatres with bars and

---

* No responsible licensee wishes people to drink more than they need or want. All he is concerned with is to see that they take their total requirements in his house rather than in that of his competitor.

beer tents at garden parties, as well as any place where drinking is done in a manner which is not social. It also excludes clubs. It would be a fascinating exercise to explore the frontiers of this distinction, and some peripheral cases will be mentioned in the pages which follow: but it is desirable first to establish our norm before considering departures from it.

Quite bluntly, there is no mystique about social drinking. Pubs are full of little quirks of convention and behaviour, but at bottom the matter is fairly simple. People drink with each other because they like to do so, and the relationships between the drinker and his environment are quite straightforward. A study of the pub in literature, and of the way it has been used throughout its history, reveals that possibly for two millennia or even longer, the same attitudes have at all times been considered significant. During this time, by a system of trial and error and by sensitive adjustment, the pub and the law controlling it have evolved together, providing a uniquely beneficial framework within which the same characteristics are encouraged and social drinking may be enjoyed, while a complex system of subtle checks discourages potential abuses. It is hardly surprising that this process has resulted in what is probably the most civilised social-drinking environment yet produced anywhere.

The relationships involved are set out in Chapter 3. They are five in number, and I believe that once the qualities which they imply are understood we shall be better able to ensure survival of the true pub, which is agreed by so many to be worth having and worth copying. This is all the more important in view of pressure from those who would like to see all distinctions lost and the pub absorbed into an amorphous leisure industry along with bingo halls, bubble-gum, hunting, shooting, fishing and football.

Part I

UNDERSTANDING THE PUB

1 The Historical Background

Pubs as we know them today are in the direct line of descent from two distinct ancestors – the inn and the tavern. The way they have evolved, and the ways in which they are still used, represent a tradition unbroken since the days of the Roman occupation. It is not that there has been no change, but the process of change has been a continous one, the two separate lines of development merging in the 19th century to become the pub, neither inn nor tavern, but partaking of the recognisable characteristics of both.

The Inn and its Origins

The word 'inn' originally meant 'a chamber', or 'a set of chambers', but there are said to be four definitions in law which agree that an inn is a place for wayfaring men. Inns have always been for the entertainment of people who travel from place to place, rather than for local residents. In these days, when you can step into your car of an evening and drive off to a place 40 or 50 miles away, this is obviously a distinction without a difference, but in Roman times it was clear. The first inns of which we have records were built by the Romans beside the first roads, which they had constructed. When they left Britain there was a decline of travelling, but the inns which they left apparently survived as various kings made decrees for their better ordering. Even at this early date they were considered important enough to warrant legislation, and this is one trend which has continued.

In 1066 we were again invaded, this time by the Normans (Norsemen originally) from Normandy. We were never, of course, defeated by the French, otherwise we might have come to share their peculiar drinking habits, and the pub would have been a rather different place. As it was, the immediate effect of the Conquest was to revive travelling, and the building of roads and inns. In 1129 an ambassador from Germany wrote,
"The Inns of England are the best in Europe, those of Canterbury the best in England, and the Fountain, wherein I now lodged as handsomely as I were in the King's Palace, the best in Canterbury."

The Fountain closed in comparatively recent years, since the Second

6

World War. Canterbury, as an ecclesiastical centre, is a good example of the favourable climate for the licensed trade which was traditionally provided by the Church. Until the 20th century it had more public houses per 100 population that any other town, and it was closely followed by other cathedral cities such as Chester. Just as, on the Continent, the monasteries were among the greatest owners of vineyards, so in England the Church was among the greatest providers of inns. People who travelled during the Middle Ages, merchants, pilgrims, warriors, thieves, scholars and pedlars, were lodged according to rank, either in the Abbot's guest house, the outbuildings of the monastery, or the pilgrims' hostel. In addition, kings and noblemen travelling with large retinues were normally offered hospitality in the castle or manor house, and put up their followers in the houses of the town. Later, as roads improved, and the monasteries could not cope with the increased demand, the outhouses of the landed noblemen became inns. The Lords of the Manor began to retire to more secluded country seats, and left behind stewards whose duty was to entertain guests. Sometimes an inn was built for this purpose, and the steward in due course was supplanted by the innkeeper. The sign of the Manor remained, giving the inn its name. The clergy, too, who had been accustomed to put up travellers in the rectory, sometimes preferred to build an inn, which remained under the control of the Church and kept up the monastic tradition of hospitality. Even today we find there is no mutual incompatibility between the church and the pub. They grew up together. The architect Sir Edwin Lutyens said; "The Church is to the spirit as the inn is to the flesh, and, if good and well designed, they baulk the Devil himself".

Mediaeval inns had galleried storeys about a central courtyard, around which the whole life of the inn revolved. Merchants displayed their goods there, and actors performed plays. It could be said with some truth that the inn was the first shop and the first theatre. Throughout the history of the pub it has fulfilled numerous functions which afterwards branched off into quite separate establishments. If this had not happened, the distinctive character which is the subject of this study might have become distorted. As it is, there is an unbroken line of development and tradition, which is flexible enough to adjust to changes without, on the one hand, being twisted out of recognition, or on the other, becoming fossilised through failure to adapt itself to the needs of the present. A large part of the technique of running pubs should be an ability to distinguish between developments which are or are not compatible with this special character, viewed as a unique commercial asset. In his book, *The English Inn* published in 1931, Thomas Burke wrote that it is always the aim of a 'landlord' to make his inn an inn of its time.

The reign of Queen Elizabeth I saw the introduction, in 1550, of what are now known as 'permitted hours'. There was a closing time of 9 o'clock in summer and 8 o'clock in winter. But it was during the Civil War and the Protectorate – a sort of Puritan dictatorship – the whole trade suffered a severe setback. In view of what has already been said it should perhaps be noted that this was an act of rebels, and that the Church remained on the side of human enjoyment for ordinary people, keeping asceticism for revered specialists. However, this sombre period came to an end, and after the Plague of London a fresh revival of trade brought increased travelling and the Golden Age of the Inn, the days of coaching. Many new inns were built and existing ones improved. This process continued throughout the 18th century, and the graceful Georgian inn was evolved of which numerous fine examples survive.

Mention of hotels brings us to the 19th century, the coming of the railways and the Railway Hotel. One cannot but admire the grandeur and munificence of the Victorian hotel. Certainly it was not a pub. It had a kind of spaciousness which belongs to a different category of enjoyment. This is, of course, yet another example of an unsuitable function being passed on, as it were, to a different institution. The inns were, in any case, in the wrong places, and they were also too small to cope with the greatly increased demand for rooms which came with the extension of travel to all classes, made possible by the railways. Consequently, the inns fell upon evil days. Deserted by coach travellers they fell back on the local trade, and thus we see the beginning of the end of the distinction between the inn as a place for wayfarers and the tavern as a resort for local people. Both became pubs, and the accommodation of travellers passed to a large extent into the rather different territory of the hotel.

The Tavern and its Origins

The tavern, meanwhile, had been following its parallel road. Always the inhabitants of England have preferred a drink and good cheer in company to private toping within the home. From Roman times, this is the function which taverns performed. The Romans called them either 'tabernae' or 'bibulia' – a word which cannot help but seem appropriate to us as applied to places where the bibulous enjoy their boozing!

In the Middle Ages, while the inns for lack of travellers were somewhat eclipsed, we hear more of taverns, and in Piers Plowman tales are told of convivial gatherings in the alehouse. By the reign of Edward VI there were as many as 40 taverns in London, and at that time they were specifically defined as being, "for the leisure hours of those around them". The tavern was the true local. The inn sign of today is a relic of the bush or bunch of grapes which was hung outside the tavern to attract the attention of illiterate customers.

A city tavern of the 15th century is described as, "a many-gabled building with numerous rooms, furnished with stools and benches and decorated with rich carving", while in the country an alehouse was thus described, "The proportions are diminutive, the timbering almost extravagant in its scantling, the fireplace in the tap room seems large enough to accommodate a crowd, while the woodwork of the high-backed settles, no less than the surface of the roughly plastered walls, indicate a finish by contact, unnoticed and unintentional."

The 16th century was the time of the stage waggons, and the waggoners had neither the social status nor the means to lodge in the inns. Indeed, it is not entirely clear where they did lodge. Probably some tavern-keepers used to put them up, for we find legislation against this practice. In any case, it was certainly in the taverns that they spent their spare time away from home, and they, together with other humble folk, were entertained in the tavern kitchen. The landlord kept his private parlour for accommodating the drinking gentry, and this distinction was, of course, the origin of the two-bar pub. The public bar, tap room, vault or vaults is the direct descendant of the tavern kitchen, while the saloon bar or smoke room is the successor of the private parlour, with its greater physical comfort and its extra pennies on a pint of beer.

After the inevitable setback under Cromwell, the Restoration brought a revival of tavern life – "all ranks and conditions of people gathered there for every conceivable social purpose. It was a rendezvous, a business office, a postal address. Professional men and court officials were 'to be heard' of at such and such a tavern. Men went there to sit in the warmth, to read, to gossip and to smoke". Debating societies and sportsmen used it as head-quarters. It was a common meeting-ground, a club open to strangers, a centre of the life of the local community.

Indeed, as has been mentioned on another page, one of the advantages of a pub over a club is precisely that it is "open to strangers" – one is not cut off from the life of the town. Absolutely anybody *may* come in. When any pub is invaded and monopolised by an exclusive clique who behave in a surly manner towards a chance customer, it is in danger of losing something valuable. This is in fact exactly what happened to some taverns in the 18th century. Attracted by the atmosphere of warmth and good-fellowship that they found there, the wits and men of letters, the intelligentsia of the time, began to use the taverns as meeting places. Addison, Goldsmith, Dr Johnson were all great frequenters of taverns. So far so good. But it appears that some of these cliques and coteries began to resent the intrusion of strangers into the particular tavern they had come to regard as their own. Observe what happened. Instead of this tendency being allowed to spoil the tavern, it was pushed to one side – the exclusive regulars made themselves into clubs and obtained premises of their own, where they could enjoy each other's company undisturbed. The fact that a few specific taverns were, in the process, lost by being purchased and converted into clubs did not affect the issue. All the rest were freed from the threat of exclusiveness, and continued as before with all the distinctive and peculiar characteristics which made them what they were. The departure of the literary people may have robbed them of some trade for a while, but surely this was better than that they should have been grossly transformed. Gradually the tavern came to be used mainly by those with no social pretensions, but it retained its own flavour, and its function as a centre of local life.

The Emergence of the Pub

There is a story of an old man who, with wisdom of age, said, "In the good old days men did not go into a public house to drown their wits in gin but to buy each other good wholesome ale in Christian fellowship. And, as every man went to church, of course, there had to be many alehouses."

From this old fellow's use of the phrase "public house", and from his reference to the alehouse as he used to know it "in the good old days" when everyone went to church, it would seem that he was living in the 19th century, in the evil days of cheap foreign gin. Gin, which was introduced to this country in the reign of William and Mary, must already have been regarded as a menace by Hogarth, whose *Gin Lane* and *Beer Alley* well illustrate the same point: but it was not until the industrial revolution that its social effects became intolerable. It was also at this time that the inns and taverns were combining their traditions to form that of the pub; the time of the coming of the railways, and the great explosion of population from 20 million to 40 million in the space of a few years. This, of course, gave rise to appalling conditions of squalor in the towns where the working masses lived and drank. Indeed, drink they did. It cannot even have been particularly good for trade, because with gin at a penny a large portion, the customers must have died off pretty fast. As far as one can judge from cartoons of the time, and making allowance for the fact that these were anti-drink propaganda, it does seem that many of the results of cheap gin really were vicious.

What had gone wrong? First, the English working people had been weaned away from their traditional ale and beer on to the Continental spirit. Secondly, they were living in a shocking state of poverty and discomfort, and needed escape. But there was a third contributory factor which arose directly out of the government's efforts to check the abuse. To encourage the drinking of beer by allowing it to be sold without a licence the 1830 Beer Act was passed.

Cottage beerhouses were opened everywhere, and many of those who kept them used to brew their own beer. Naturally the larger brewing concerns took exception to this. The only way they could hit back was by concentrating on the licensed houses, which alone could sell gin. So the brewers began to buy pubs and to build new ones, originating in the process the Gin Palace – the grand Victorian corner pub, or 'boozer'. Like the term 'boozer' which was applied to it, this was largely a metropolitan type, and it was the result, not the cause, of the gin habit which had affected the multitude. It must, indeed, have aggravated the very evil which the government had hoped to combat. In the long run this operated very much to the disadvantage of the pub, which from that time began to fall into social disrepute, while much of the goodwill upon which the trade had ultimately to depend was dissipated. The publican himself came to be looked upon less as a friend than as a 'governor' – the kind of ruling personage who took your money and kicked you out. Even today, after more than a century's progress back to normal, there are people in London and elsewhere who still look on the licensee and his pub as something not quite respectable.

That pubs of this period, both architecturally and as drinking places, can be a stimulating success is now widely accepted, but in its time the Gin Palace was undoubtedly frowned upon by Nice People. The Temperance faction, needless to say, took a not altogether unjustified advantage of the situation. Who could blame them if they played it up as hard as they could. In 1910 H. P. Maskell, an architect and a great champion of the pub, wrote, "If the Public House fails to realise its ideal as the expression of Christian charity and social freedom, the fault is with the Pharisees, fanatics and sectaries who seek by all the methods of chicanery to ruin and defame it." It was, in fact, true that at that time the Temperance people opposed any and every attempt to reform or improve the pub, thinking that the worse it was the better it suited their purpose of introducing the arch-evil of prohibition.

So it was not until the First World War that anything useful could be done to haul the pub up out of the slough of despond into which it had fallen. Abnormal conditions among munition workers at Gretna caused the government to step in, and the Liquor Control Board took over all the licensed houses in the area. This was the 'Carlisle Experiment', and it was the beginning of state-owned pubs in the Carlisle district . It was also the first step towards the 'Improved Public House' movement, which after the war was taken up by the brewers. One may have doubts whether the pubs it produced were 'improved' in any but a narrow architectural sense, but it was clear that something had to be done to rescue the pub from its parlous state and re-establish it in the esteem of the public. As far as this goes, the efforts then made, together with the changed social conditions between the Wars, were on the whole successful in that the stigma which had been attached to pub-going did decline.

All this happened in a period when the population was re-distributed, increased use of the roads in motor cars and char-a-bancs led town people into the countryside to discover the little old pubs which had remained unchanged: women, emancipated by the War and by the Suffrage Act, began to invade the pubs, and millions of people who had never done so before became customers.

The Pub from 1920 to the Present Day

A brewery company once described their policy of Improved Public Houses thus. It meant "the pulling down and large-scale reconstruction of antiquated houses: the building of new houses on much more ambitious lines, with larger rooms and lounges in place of narrow and congested bars. It meant the re-equipment of the public house with modern furniture and schemes of decoration, and the introduction of the most up-to-date methods of lighting and ventilation. It meant the addition of assembly halls, games rooms and children's rooms. The new local was altogether a larger, cleaner and brighter establishment with good architecture without and good decorative taste within."

Small wonder that faithful customers, who had loved the old pubs as they were, tended to view such a policy with distrust and accepted its results with distaste. The reasons for its failure are summed up by Maurice Gorham and H. Mc G. Dunnett, from whose book *Inside The Pub*, published by The Architectural Press in 1950, the following quotations are taken:

"The pubs went Tudor and embraced all the incongruities inevitable when sterilised mediaeval frills are draped round 20th century mass-production and amenities. It was a formula which bore no relation to . . . the true functional tradition of the pub."

"When pseudo styles were cast to one side . . . the choice seems to have been either a modernistic model of about 1930 which long ago looked tawdry and dated . . . completely characterless, or an edition of modernised Georgian . . . which has been labelled the 'Post Office' style (and) particularly emphasised the bare, bleak interior."

"It is apparent that the pubs evolved by the brewers and their architects during the 20 years between the Wars have not embodied the qualities that we find in many of the older pubs and which we would like to see reflected in the new. Instead they are bleak, impersonal, barrack-like or pompous and self-conscious, and lacking in intimacy or bonhomie."

Sir James Richards, in his foreword to the same book, wrote, "The things that are important about pub interiors are, on the whole, quite independent of the architectural styles current when they were built. A good Tudor pub is not good on account of its black oak beams and the leaded lights in its windows, any more than a good Victorian pub is good simply on account of its carved mahogany screens and the engraved glass in its windows. In spite of their superficial differences, they are both good because of what they have in common, rather than because of what links them with one particular period . . . The things they have in common, the methods used to create a sense of warmth and friendliness in old pubs, – of whatever period – are equally valid today. The close and intricate subdivision of large rooms to give a feeling of seclusion and intimacy, the use of glass screens and mirrors to give mystery and sparkle, the use of rich, dark colours, the use of bottles and barrels and Brewers' trade marks as decoration. These can all be legitimately used in modern designs to build anew upon whatever remains valid of the old."

His words did not go unheeded. At Ind Coope and Allsopps in Burton-upon-Trent during the early 1950's there was a group of architects whose good fortune it was to work under Neville G. Thompson as Technical Director and Carl Fairless (later Jim Witham) as Chief Architect: but they enjoyed another advantage. In wartime there had been little else to do but drink in one's spare time, so they had actually used pubs – a privilege apparently denied to many of their predecessors. Thus, they were able to appreciate the wisdom of Richards, Gorham and Dunnett, and the book became a 'bible' for them and for their colleagues in London, Oxford, Cardiff, Burslem, and Leeds.

An Ind Coope Vault of the 1950's. Surfaces were all of teak except the curved wall which was covered with dark green leather-cloth, and the ceiling which was high gloss midnight-blue on crystal-structure anaglypta. The metalwork was polished brass

Being specialists in pubs they were able to produce interiors more human, more traditional and more sympathetic for their purpose than the great bulk of work in this field between the two World Wars. They developed something which was almost a style, the traces of which can still be recognised in a scattering of pubs from Gateshead to Gwent. The bareness and bleakness of the 1930's bars were replaced with an appearance both more intimate and less institutional. Rooms were often deliberately twisted into angular shapes, or the fixtures and fittings were planned to achieve this effect. There were areas of low ceiling, generally finished with polished timber boarding, a material which was also used on walls and counter fronts. Another popular element was polished copper on counter tops and tables. The use of anaglypta was revived, and a special pattern was produced based on 1951 Festival of Britain 'crystal structure' wallpaper designs. Walls were covered with dark-coloured leathercloth, and sometimes lettering was used as decoration. Ray Carter designed special ranges of cast-iron tables, with timber tops, and timber stools and chairs. The whole 'style', if such it was, returned for its inspiration to the essentials of 'pubness', and catered for the customers' psychological needs in a way seldom previously encountered in 20th century pubs.

13

An Ind Coope Smoke Room of the 1950's. Ceiling, walls and floor were all of teak, the counter front was terrazzo in darkish green, and the top was polished copper. There was some purple carpet in an alcove

An Ind Coope Public Bar of the 1950's. The colouring was mainly browns and tans with natural timber

The 1950's additions blend in well with the original detail

The value of this achievement in terms of customer-satisfaction and of cash in the till has gone largely unacknowledged to this day by the Trade, but other designers were more appreciative, adopting many of the Ind Coope components into their own work. Unfortunately it seems that, unless they specialise, architects often fail to solve the particular problems involved in the creation of a social drinking atmosphere. Their training ill equips them for designing pubs, because it tends to instil a somewhat limited and stilted approach. Even some of those architects who are prepared to tackle a pub interior are still affected by the sterile aftermath of the Modern Movement – a sort of bareness and austerity. They tend to base their work too firmly on the T-square, and in this they are abetted by the quantity surveyor, quick to point out that straight lines and right angles are cheaper to build than irregular spaces, and forgetting that when such attitudes are successfully resisted the results are time and again justified by trade figures.

Of course, during this period mistakes were made, especially by those who were trying to follow a good example without fully understanding its nature. A case in point was the inflation of the 'Theme' into the 'Gimmick'.

15

A 20th century interior which retains the tradition: only the counter front remains of the original 1930s fixtures

A good designer, wishing to get away from the sameness of most Thirties' pubs and some modern ones, would occasionally seize on the name of a house, and use it as a theme for choosing incidental embellishments. This fairly innocuous process got out of hand. Commercial firms in the pub decorating business, encouraged by certain brewery commercial staff, indulged in every kind of extravagant absurdity in the invention of gimmicks, racking their brains to think of a new nonsense whenever a pub was built or an existing bar renovated. The atlas was combed from Spain to the South Seas, the compendium of trades and occupations from whaling to wheel-tapping, the sporting calendar from ice-hockey to hurling. A bar must, never, on any account, look like a bar, "What should we make it look like instead?".

The misconception here was a simple one. Abolishing the bareness and bleakness was seen to work. Because customers preferred warmth and visual incident to the cold, clinical look, the well-designed post-War bars were a commercial success: but would-be copyists, appreciating only the superficial effect without realising the underlying philosophy, discovered that it was difficult to find a source, a vocabulary of ornament unless they were provided with a gimmick to spark off their imagination. The Modern

To an architect this appears as an uneasy mixture of archaic and modern, but it works

Movement and the so-called functional approach to design had impoverished the visual language. So, dimly understanding what had to be done, but having no ready means of doing it, they cast about them for ideas, and latched upon any irrelevant idiocy, even introducing such things as trees and running water to the indoor scene.

In doing so, many of them missed, at any rate for a number of years, the reservoir of visual richness, the ready-made tradition which was under their collective nose, the existing residue of Victorian and Edwardian pubs. Admittedly, the attitudes of the 'Twenties and 'Thirties had been all against such places. Possibly the evil days of gin with which they were associated were fresh in people's minds. The horrors of modernisation were inflicted on too many 19th-century pubs, and those which remained were so despised by their owners that very few were lovingly maintained. Before and during World War II most of them were allowed to fall into a state of dismal squalor, which led to a vague feeling in the public mind that they were 'not quite nice'. However, in the 1960's, more and more people, including the gimmick merchants, came to recognise their merits. Brewers' Victoriana succeeded Brewers' Tudor as the fashionable style of the day. Instant-pub package-dealers churned out their standard pastiche by the

17

A few examples of Victorian and Edwardian detail

18

19

kilometre. It must be admitted that in the process they achieved some quite acceptable drinking places. This was only to be expected: but unfortunately they seemed unaware of the need, in every period, to build something new on the foundation of tradition, and forgot that, especially in pubs, tradition is broken when development and change come to a halt. Among the people who avoided this trap were Roderick Gradidge, whose interest in the Arts and Crafts movement gave his imaginative work a sound basis, and Michael Jacks, whose uncomprisingly modern designs went back to even earlier sources for their inspiration. Roy Wilson Smith also managed to get away from the general dull dependence on 1930's models, and we can learn a great deal from at least one aspect of his interiors. A typical Wilson Smith alteration resulted in a complex of interlocking, overlapping, interpenetrating three-dimensional spaces, connected by short flights of shallow steps leading off at every angle and in all directions. The details of finishes and furnishings were less successful, however, and although his work owed more to tradition than he might admit, his method appeared to depend on the complete gutting of an existing building, leaving nothing perceptible of the original interior. In this, of course, he was by no means alone. Far too often the sort of elaboration and enrichment appropriate and needful when applied to most pubs of the 1930's has been forced instead on earlier houses, and in the process we have lost many fine panelled counter fronts, moulded counter nosings, matchboard dadoes, good timber floors, elegant but unassuming built-in furniture. The wheel, in fact, has come full circle. The danger now is not that 'Thirties bars will be left in their original bleakness, but that bars of earlier periods with a high degree of sound, honest-to-goodness pub quality will be over-lushed-up, for no better reason than that someone has let them get superficially shabby, and the man in charge can neither see nor appreciate their solid merit.

As far as the grander type of 19th century pub is concerned, its re-establishment in popular regard is now fully assured. In the 1970's Brian Spiller and Mark Girouard wrote their excellent books on the Victorian pub, and already some brewers have begun to carry out sensitive restorations. Tetleys have initiated in Liverpool their 'Heritage Inns' exercise, rescuing among others the famous Philharmonic and The Vines (better known to Scouse regulars as The Big House). An equally impressive job has been made of the Central. It must not be forgotten that unless such a policy shows what the brewers regard as a proper return, they will drop it like a hot potato, and to my mind it is better, with absolute respect for the spirit of the architecture, to ensure that the finished job will appeal to the customers, rather than to follow the art historians too slavishly.

New pubs built in the 1960's and 1970's are, not surprisingly, a pretty mixed bunch. To undertake a serious survey would be an agreeable but time-consuming research, and until it is undertaken the value of comment on a random selection is limited. However, I have the impression that, in general, achievement has been very considerable. Probably first in the field of private architects designing good pub interiors were Mayell Hart and

20

Partners, but others followed, and now it can be said that not every new pub consists of two rectangular bars;* not every bar's ceiling is a uniform plane 3.5 m above floor level. Pubs are still built which are dull and depressing: others have erred in the opposite direction by trying too hard to startle and to strike attitudes: but many are sympathetic arrangements of space, sympathetically finished and furnished. The criticism frequently levelled at the Trade, that all new pubs are horrible, is no longer true.

To choose one example, the City of London Yeoman at Fenchurch Street, London, is a multi-level labyrinth of spaces contrived by Ind Coope's Romford architects (with John Gammans in charge of the job) in the basement of a new office block. Without being ostentatious in any way, and without deliberate 'period' styling, the designer has drawn upon limited aspects of the 19th century vocabulary of materials and forms to produce an interior which is neither pastiche nor gimmick, yet escapes the insipidity of so much 'modern' architecture. The result, to my mind, deserves high marks for its spatial qualities, the treatment of surfaces: choice of furnishings and comfortable artificial lighting. Would that all owners of pubs would provide us, the drinking public, with environments as satisfying and acceptable in new pubs.

* Some were indeed laid out in that way by Douglas Shepherd in the 1960's, but still managed, by means of materials, colours and lighting, to present a 'drinkable' appearance.

2 The Essence Of 'Pubness'

The quality of 'Pubness' is the total theme of this book. As might be expected of an architect I have dealt at length with the attributes of space, of surfaces, of contents and of lighting. Speaking more as a customer I also make the point that polish is needed, not only to enhance the appearance of everything by reflecting light, but in order to convey a sense that the place, and therefore the people using it, are well cared for. If all these things are present and correct to the nth degree, there will be a pub of high quality which, other things being equal, will trade well. However, there are two other characteristics which belong to some of the very best pubs, which are sought after by many, and which can be regarded as a useful bonus, though strictly speaking they are not really essential to a first rate drinking environment.

'Authenticity' is the first of these. It is hard to describe because it is something one experiences rather than sees. It implies a kind of coherence, an easy relationship of the parts with each other and with the whole. It is most often, but by no means exclusively found in older pubs. Basil Sugden and others have produced Public Bars which are modern and yet possess a high degree of authenticity. One essential is that there should be nothing in an 'authentic' bar which is obviously contrived or false. I say 'obviously' because a carefully contrived 'falsehood' can be totally imperceptible and therefore acceptable. Certainly the feeling of authenticity will be dispersed by the introduction of anything perversely and blatantly out of place, sticking out like the proverbial sore thumb: and I suggest that it may also be true that furnishing items newer than the building are far less likely to produce a disturbing effect than pieces which are older. It is a natural process for new things to be added with the passing of time, and if they are sensitively chosen no harm is done, but the self-conscious addition of antiques and period fittings into a new bar may well deprive it of this quality.

'Design flair' is the second valuable but non-essential characteristic. It is given by those designers who have it to give, and it carries with it a sense of

22

surprise as well as of delight. Surprise without delight is of course not enough. Delight with no sense of surprise is naturally to be welcomed and enjoyed, but it does not in itself constitute 'design flair', which is the product of a more than usually creative imagination.

Here is my suggested list of the environmental factors for which a man (or a woman) looks, whether consciously or not – the feelings which he likes to enjoy when he goes into a pub:

1. He likes to feel welcome

This is the relationship between the customer and the licensee. We find in good pubs a sort of welcome which is more personal than that normally offered by a grocer or a bank manager. The licensee is as much a friend as a tradesman. He extends hospitality, even to strangers, of a kind which transcends the purely commercial situation. He welcomes us into his own home, in much the same way as his predecessor received the humble waggoner into his kitchen and the gentry into his parlour. Despite the fact that nowadays a pub may be a lock-up shop the relationship between 'mine host' and his guests can still exist, and is appreciated. *Warmth* is the word which is commonly used to describe a welcome, and this hint should be remembered by the designer.

2. He likes to feel at home

This is the relationship between the customer and the pub itself. Once he has been made welcome a guest must then be made to feel 'at home' in the sense that he does not feel '*out of place*'. He has taken cover from something, whether it is the youngsters or the old folks, the heat or the cold, or merely the strains and stresses of the outside world. If he is in any way exposed, isolated or vulnerable, he will feel uneasiness, and he will depart whether or not he is consciously aware of the source of such feelings. What he requires is a sense of *seclusion*, and this is one way in which the designer can make a significant contribution.

3. He likes to give and to enjoy friendliness

This is the relationship between the customer and other customers. The pub and its predecessors, the tavern and the inn, have always been regarded as the place above all for good fellowhip, definitely not for formal behaviour. One dosen't wish to feel that one should straighten one's tie. Primness and rigidity give place to relaxation, stimulation and conversation. As Nikolaus Pevsner said, "The function of the pub is company, human nearness, . . . snugness not smugness." In a word, it is *informality* that is required, and here again the designer has his part to play.

4. He likes a goodhearted atmosphere

This is the relationship between the customer and all the world. It is something rather more abstract than good fellowship. In their book, *Old Country Inns* published in 1912, H. P. Maskell and E. W. Gregory expressed

23

it by saying that, "The keynote of the public house and its true purpose in life is Christian Charity". A good pub reflects the best, not the worst in human values, and in it the spirit should be able to expand rather than suffer restriction or distortion. This quality may well have stemmed from the ancient and traditional connection between Church and Pub, which long before the Reformation arose from the natural order of things; but I use here the word *goodheartedness*, with which non-Christians need not disagree. Nevertheless, a clear distinction must be made between the guffaw and the snigger – between good natured ribaldry or honest bawdiness on the one hand – (which are part of the scene), and more sophisticated forms of nastiness and depravity (which are not) on the other.

5. He likes a sense of continuity
This is the relationship between the customer and history. Pubs appeal to the Englishman's instinct of permanence. But it should be remembered that true tradition looks both ways, forward as well as back. It is not concerned solely with the past. The pub's tradition is one of continual change, and it is no paradox to say that when it ceases to change it will lose touch with tradition. One basic satisfaction of the ancient custom of social drinking is to feel at one with those who have enjoyed it in the past and also those who will enjoy it (possibly, though not necessarily, here in this very bar . . .) in the future. Change, though continuous, must therefore be gradual enough to ensure that the pub remains recognisable because it is *in certain essentials familiar*. Otherwise the process of tradition can be broken and its value lost. In the past designers, as well as management, have too often been guilty of neglecting this fact.

What I am suggesting is that the reason for the pub's undoubted social and commercial success, and the reason why it has become the envy of those who don't have it, is simply that more often than not it has managed to offer to the customer all or most of these five relationships which he requires between himself and the various aspects of his drinking environment. To depart from the values implied in them may give some financial success in the short term, but in the long run it will fail. This has been true at all times. It is less easy to demonstrate that it is also true in all places; but if there is a part of the world where people like to feel unwelcome, out of place, stiffly formal, if there is a place where ill-humour is preferred to kindness and where men disregard the continuum of time, there I will admit that my claim does not apply. It seems unlikely that in such a place there would be any social drinking.

All these reflections are extremely simple: the subtleties start, however, when one tries to convert them into a three-dimensional statement with open doors through which we can all stroll at opening time amd be served with drinks. It must be asked, what is the connection between these relationships and the design of the place? My answer is, that the connection is one of feeling. A feeling is a state of mind, and our state of mind is affected

24

by our surroundings. The atmosphere created affects the state of mind of the customers – the way they feel – and this in turn affects the length of time they remain and also the chances that they will return. If it is true, then, that customers in pubs like to feel 'goodhearted', at one with history, friendly, welcome, not out of place, then the design must not be antagonistic to any of these feelings. If it is, they will leave in search of another drinking place, probably without quite knowing why – their reaction is based on a subconscious assessment of the surroundings. This, then, is not only the connection between the five relationships and the design. It is also the connection between the design and the commercial success of the pubs we build or improve.

The problem, therefore, is how to express in architectural or visual terms the sort of interior which will encourage rather than inhibit the enjoyment of social drinking; but first we must examine and enumerate the visual qualities possessed by interiors in general, and then go on to relate them to our special needs, the particular requirements of a social drinking environment.

The characteristics of any enclosed volume, be it cave, cupboard or cathedral, may be defined by reference to its architectural qualities, which are:

1. Its three-dimensional shape, that is, its *spatial qualities*
2. The nature of the enclosing and sub-dividing *surfaces*
3. The *contents* built or brought into it, and
4. The natural and artificial *lighting*

In this way the problem can be broken down into its components, and each can be considered in turn, organised, controlled and chosen in order to achieve the desired effect, whatever may be the intended function of the interior. For instance, a simple 'rectangular' room (which is not, incidentally, a good drinking space) is a cuboid. Its *spatial quality* is regulated by its length, breadth and height. Its enclosing *surfaces* are the ceiling, walls and floor, together with any doors and windows. There may in addition be subdividing fixtures and screens. The *contents* will include all fixed and loose furniture and every article placed in the room. Our description is completed by the assessment of the quality, intensity, colour and distribution of *light sources*. A social drinking place (or indeed any other) may thus be specified in terms of what is desirable in the way of space, surfaces, contents and lighting for its purpose. My specification in the following chapters does, in fact, constitute an extended brief rather than a solution, since the intention here is to indicate what should be aimed at, leaving the designer to achieve it in his own way.

3 Spatial Qualities

Although people like to feel 'at home' in a pub, in the sense that they do not feel out-of-place, this by no means implies that we can make a pub resemble any particular person's home – it is not a matter of reproducing what we find in other people's houses. A customer does not use a pub in quite the same way as he does his home. He uses it more as a home *from* home, as a kind of extension or annex, sometimes even as an escape from the home, or at any rate from some of the people there. He therefore likes to feel that he is voluntarily cut off, possibly from certain people, certainly from the world outside. It is not that he is an escapist exactly – he remains a free agent, and when he has been fortified and strengthened by a couple of pints it may well be his intention to walk out again. Meanwhile, what he will enjoy is a sense of *seclusion*. He does not want to feel isolated or conspicuous, all alone in the middle of an acreage of bare floor space. This is why 'narrow and congested bars' (as someone once, with small understanding, derogatorily called them) are so popular. However, it is impracticable always to provide a multitude of small bars, since these cause insuperable difficulties of circulation, ventilation and staffing. So the designer must find means of providing, in large areas, the sense of seclusion which is demanded.

He has to create illusions which will do away with any feeling of excessive, open, uninterrupted space. Indeed, vacant floor space, as well as making customers feel isolated, exposed and as it were vulnerable, are commercially uneconomical. Subdivision is therefore needed, but here it must be remembered that a room whose proportion is horizontal always feels more comfortable, and gives a greater sense of repose, than a tall vertical one, like a cell, which intimidates and dwarfs the occupant. A space which has been divided by building solid partitions up to the ceiling is nothing but a series of such vertical compartments. Subdivision must therefore be done in such a way as to maintain the horizontal proportion of the space which is subdivided. In many Victorian pubs this was achieved by means of transparent screens which did not reach to the ceiling. Not only was the drinker conscious of continuing space seen through the decorative glazing, but over the tops of the partitions he could see the ceiling common to all the compartments, and thus apprehend something of the extent of the place. He was aware of the fact that its overall proportion, despite its considerable height, gave in fact a horizontal rather than a vertical shape, and so he could enjoy simultaneously the reposefulness of the whole and the seclusion of the part – the relatively small subdivision or 'bar', whether Public, Private or Saloon, which he had entered. This had the added advantage that although he was sufficiently enclosed to feel protected and inconspicuous, he could still participate in the life of the place, and he was not deprived of the chance of hearing a friend's voice in the next cubby-hole, and walking round to join him for a pint and a chat.

I am not, of course, suggesting that Victorian architects deliberately set out to achieve such happy effects. Their multi-compartmented interiors were the result of social divisions very different from those of today. Nevertheless they worked and, learning from them, we can nowadays apply other devices in order to provide semi-secluded areas within the general seclusion of the whole pub, rather than the total fragmentation which is no longer required. Members of convivial groups of customers do not wish to be cut off from each other, and neither do they wish to lose all connection with the rest of the crowd. Their small group forms part of the larger one which is everyone there. The concept of the semi-secluded space is a delicate one, and the precise degree of separation needs to be carefully arranged. In practice it is regulated to some extent by the necessity to supervise all such areas from behind the counter, normally insisted on by Licensing Benches if not by licensees.

It is worth noting here that a partition, though it punctuates the floor space, occupies very little area in itself. Nothing is wasted. On the contrary, it forms boundaries or *intermediate limits* against which people may sit or stand. Without such a limit to lean on, or at any rate to relate to, they feel discomfort and exposure, so they gravitate to the edge, or into a corner. Corners *are*, in fact, semi-secluded areas, and the more of them there are, the better, up to a point. When for all practical purposes this point is reached it is still possible to subdivide space in other ways, for instance, by means of changes of level in the ceiling, or in the floor, or in both, in which case an interesting complexity is possible within the permutations: ceiling up, floor down; ceiling up, floor up; ceiling down, floor up; ceiling down, floor down. A modest post and rail can visually enclose a corner, and a series of posts with rails returning to the wall provides a row of alcoves. In every case, the aim must be to provide a degree of seclusion without physical restriction or any sense of imprisonment. The customer is content to be aware that he has *come* in, without feeling *shut* in. There is a difference between being enfolded and being encased; between going to one's bed and being put in one's coffin. It is dull and disturbing to be shut in a box, but in a labyrinth of caves there is an element of excitement as well as of safety. One can wander about exploring. The precise boundaries of a cave are irregular, and seldom immediately noticeable. It is enough to know they are there.

There may, indeed, be some deep connection between this idea and the race-memory of the cave as man's original refuge from the perils of prehistoric life: it does seem to be true that one of the satisfactions sought in the pub is that of being enclosed, relaxed and protected, and the notion of one's drinking place as a cave can give us several clues about the sort of space which will be successful. A certain irregularity of layout can enhance one's comfort by adding informality to seclusion. Not all the angles need be 90 degrees, not all the lines straight. If they are, there will be an appearance of rigidity, and much of the effect achieved by screens and alcoves and changes of level will be neutralised. It is not really difficult to see why a simple shape is by no means satisfactory. Because every part of it can be seen at once, it follows that a customer within it can be observed from every point. This makes him feel conspicuous. Exposure and vulnerability are accentuated. Existing rooms of this kind therefore present a problem. Irregularly planned subdivisions may not be feasible, or even if they are they may not be enough. However, by using large framed mirrors we can penetrate walls, make solid screens transparent and give an impression of complexity. A continuous row of mirrors just below the top of a wall can make a tall room appear more horizontal. Few drinking areas are happier than a complex of loosely interconnected spaces, and where this does not exist in truth the appearance of it is a good substitute. It can remove the sense of restriction and of being boxed in. The position of the room's apparent limits is disguised and its edges blurred. An acme of success in this kind of illusion is reached when a hole in the wall is mistaken for a mirror, and vice versa! Nothing but harm has been done by those brewery directors of 'taste' who have had mirrors removed on the ground that they are rather vulgar. If they had done their homework they would have learned from John Piper, who wrote in his *Buildings and Prospects* in 1948, that the pub needs its "trace-element of vulgarity to keep it lusty". As all illusionists know, mirrors are magic, and this is no less true when dealing with the spatial qualities of bars.

The sense of having taken cover is non-existent if the windows are too big. If there is truth in my suggestion about caves, it may be significant that the mouth of a cave is usually its only window: but it does *have* a mouth, which represents its link with the outside world. This serves the dual purpose of avoiding any sense of having been trapped and at the same time accentuating one's feeling of seclusion within – it can remind us, by a fleeting glimpse, of whatever it is that we have come in to get away from, and thus adds to our satisfaction in having done so. The protection remains; but if we can be observed from outside it is largely lost. This is perhaps why, in Victorian pubs which normally had a very great area of glass, much of it was covered with decoration, etched and embossed work at least up to a passer-by's eye level, and often coloured leaded lights above, leaving a fairly narrow gap of clear glass above the standing customer's eye level through which he could see only the top of a silk hat, or of a tramcar. This rather subtle connection of space between inside and out has much in common with the semi-seclusion of internal alcoves. Both are limited and partial links. Even a Dive Bar is improved by a few small windows below the ceiling but above pavement level. I know of two or three such in London.* However, if this is not possible its lack may well be overridden by the sensation of plunging down steps 'away from it all'. As most pub-goers will have discovered in old country pubs, just a very few steps down as one enters a bar can give a similar kind of satisfaction.

A common spatial fault, especially in houses built between the two Wars, is that the customers find themselves separated from their host and his staff, looking at them as it were through a hole in the wall. This is not a welcoming arrangement. It is as though they were of a different social order, either too menial to be in the room with us, or too superior to mingle with the masses to whom they condescend to shove pints, like tickets in the station booking office. Either way it is wrong, because in a bar it should be taken for granted that all social grades are suspended while we are there. The staff greet us as friends, without obsequiousness, often with a genial rudeness which is taken and returned in good part. This is another mark of the pub as distinct from the shop, and it should not be negated by the layout of the counters or the shape of the space. How much better than a horizontal slot is the forward thrust of a counter built out into the room, enabling those serving to move towards us and among us. It is no barrier, but a link between people, a device for sociability. This indeed is a very good reason for not forming a canopy or false ceiling parallel with the counter, with a vertical upstand in the same plane as the front. Wherever this is done – and it is far too widespread – an effect very similar to the hole-in-the-wall results.

The proper use of false ceilings is to divide space, as suggested above, but if they divide customers from staff the idea of welcome can be lost. It is better to plan them in such a way that they cut *across* the line of the counter and form a visual link between the two parts of the space. A relatively minor point is that if the width of a servery is too great from back to front, even this can give an uneasy impression that we are being kept at arm's length and pushed away rather than welcomed.

To summarise the main spatial qualities which are found to provide the customer with the five relationships he needs with his pub: a horizontal rather than a vertical emphasis, boundaries irregular or confused or made to appear so, no large vacant floor areas, varying degrees of subdivision according to the type of bar, provision of semi-secluded areas within the whole, a tenuous link with the outside world from which he has escaped, an easy informality of linear expression, asymmetry, and positive visual links with those who are there to offer a friendly service. Alternatively, tiny rooms of a sort which are often very economically impracticable, can offer a great deal of what is required.

All this is merely the bare bones. A lot of architectural skill and ingenuity can be deployed in the organization of space to meet our needs as

---

* One, the Magpie and Stump, Chelsea, has recently been spoiled by an ill-conceived alteration.

social drinkers. One need not, however, use a steam hammer in order to crack nuts. The science of space subdivision is not one which demands excessive expenditure of money or material. A single column in the middle of a rectangular area divides it into four parts immediately. Christmas decorations hanging from the ceiling can transform a plain room into a grotto – though heaven forbid they should remain up all the year round – effects must be arrived at by more permanent means. Designers, if any read this book, will not thank me for dotting and crossing too many i's and t's – they are well able to search their repertoire and vocabulary of form in order to find solutions. Nevertheless, one particular spatial trick is worth mentioning as an example. It is one of which use can often be made in alterations to buildings, when a wall is knocked down to connect two rooms. First, it is both more effective and more economical to leave a projecting pier at each end, it may be as little as half a brick or as much as two and a half: and secondly, it is insensitive and ham-fisted to finish the job by putting in a straight, horizontal beam with square abutments. Arches connect spaces, lintols divide. At the very least, let us have shaped or rounded corners at the top of the new opening, or a bracket at each end (which could give an opportunity for enrichment – see Chapter 4 'Surfaces'). This way the outline is softened, allowing the visible space to flow smoothly through the opening without causing visual 'eddies' or harshness. So one may link a series of spaces more comfortably than with crudely cut rectilinear gaps, and form a labyrinth of caves in which seclusion, welcome and informal friendliness may be enjoyed.

4 Surface Treatment

In terms of space a simple box-shaped room (unless it is very small and intimate) is unsatisfactory because it gives no sense of seclusion. The faults of such a room will be aggravated if the enclosing *surfaces* obtrude too much on our attention. It is thus true in this case to say that the more obvious one makes the enclosing surfaces the less sense of seclusion results, because their plainness will reveal and accentuate the unsympathetic shape of the room. Now because the human eye is attracted by the brightest object in its field of vision, pale coloured surfaces, which reflect more light, are particularly noticeable. Our first precaution, therefore, is to choose a colour which is not too pale: some degree of sheen or gloss is also desirable, because although the shiny surface does reflect light it breaks it and scatters it, camouflaging the plainness. By contrast, flat colour throws the light back in a 'slab' of uniform tone, emphasising the blank rectangular shape of the wall. It is also necessary, in a bare, boxy room, to relieve the surfaces by means of architectural features or visual incident of some kind in addition to pattern and texture, to alleviate the bareness and provide a continuous variety of scene, enfolding the customer and maintaining his comfort. This is, in fact, a second reason why plain, blank areas of ceiling, walls or floor are at all cost to be avoided. As well as emphasising unsatisfactory shapes they form a gap in the completeness of the comfort which we wrap round ourselves during the process of social drinking. It matters little whether we regard the result of a blank space as a psychological draught whistling in through the gap, or whether we say that our warmth and cosiness is sucked out through a hole into the vacuum outside. Either way we feel exposure; our protection is pierced, and we are vulnerable.

Ceilings

Of course the worst and largest and potentially most offensive blank space in any room is the ceiling; unlike the floor it cannot be covered with furniture or people, and normally the only thing we hang from it is lighting. The worst possible treatment is to paint it white (as people used to do at one time

Horror vacui *is a complaint highly desirable for a pub designer!*

without thinking about it). A white ceiling, for optical reasons mentioned above, attracts our attention upwards, which has two ill effects. It emphasises the vertical dimension, the height of the room, thus counteracting the reposefulness of a horizontal space; and because it reflects so much light it resembles the sky, which is at once the source of natural light out of doors, and the symbol of everything we have come to avoid. All menace comes from the sky – rain, hail, lightning, thunderbolts, sunstroke, aeroplanes, birds; consequently it cannot be right to make a pub ceiling look like the sky (except perhaps in a pub frequented largely by miners or other under-ground workers). However, it is obvious that a ceiling intersected with a pattern of timbers – the 'old oak beam' variety – is already acceptable. The timbers themselves provide the visual relief which is needed. Such a ceiling in a low room, being not far above eye level, can appear very dark because the off-black joists obscure the spaces between them, and it is therefore unnecessary to apply strong colour to these interstices as well.

Victorian ceilings were patterned, not with joists and beams, but with relief decoration of (or resembling) fibrous plaster work. Some were of pressed steel, and some of patterned anaglypta. This material is a type of *papier-mâché*, made both in deeply modelled panels about 600–700 mm square, and in rolls like wallpaper much less deeply embossed. At the time of writing, anaglypta in traditional patterns is becoming less readily avail-able, but slightly smaller panels of thin plastic are being produced in some of the old designs. When painted these are hard to distinguish from the earlier product; they are also cheaper and said to be easier to fix. However, if the sheet variety finally diappears it will be difficult to replace, and the problem of the smooth plastered ceiling in a low room will be hard to deal with. It is fairly obvious that higher ceilings demand a pattern which is larger and more deeply embossed, while low relief is preferable is lower ones.

Another traditional treatment for ceilings which is very acceptable visually is tongued, grooved and bead-moulded boarding, but this may not be popular with fire authorities. In the 1950's polished hardwood boarding was often used, but this is costly and may still offend against the regulations. Patterned wallpaper (normally *not* pictorial!) finished with transparent emulsion glaze, is a possibility, or at the very least it is advisable to apply to ceilings a warm-coloured paint, preferably gloss or egg-shell rather then matt. Whatever colour is used, ceilings tend to become brown with smoke, which gives a comfortably mellow appearance: but since this process takes a few years it seems reasonable to simulate the effect from the start, which can be done either by means of plain gloss paint of a nicotine shade, or by a stippled scumble treatment akin to the brush-grain technique traditionally used on boarded dadoes and walls. This colouring of ceilings, now taken for granted in pub decoration, may well have been used in earlier days, but if so it must have been lost, with much else of value, in the early 20th century. It was re-introduced in 1954 in the White Lion Bars of the Hotel Leofric at Coventry, becoming thoroughly established a little later when regulars of the Swan and Mitre at Bromley, Kent, demanded that their richly nicotined low ceiling be reinstated after alterations. The result was a great success, because the late Dick Moorby and I, who were jointly responsible, were not permitted to pay for drinks in that bar for some years afterwards! Nowadays I would reserve a really dark tone of brown for much higher ceilings, but even low ones seem to need a touch of tan, sand or biscuit colour, to make them less harsh and noticeable, unless, as I say, this function is already performed by a pattern of joists and beams.

Cornice and Frieze

Working down from the ceiling, there may or may not be a moulded or modelled cornice, and below that a frieze, either decorative or plain, extending from the lowest moulding of the cornice down to the picture rail. The influence of the Modern Movement has resulted in the virtual disappearance of such niceties, but it is worth noting that they perform an important visual function, especially in high rooms. A cornice softens the otherwise harsh collision between horizontal and vertical surfaces, at the top of the wall; while a frieze forms a downwards extension of the ceiling, reducing the excessive scale of a high room. Let the decorative treatment acknowledge these facts, and use colours which allow a gradual transition between ceiling and wall. A shade which 'splits the difference' between ceiling and wall treatment is the obvious choice. It is also obvious that any harsh contrast in colour at this high level will attract attention upwards, with the effects I have mentioned as being undesirable in a pub. It is often tempting to make use of a cornice for introducing that touch of white or pale colour without which any colour scheme can appear dull. However (as it took me some years to discover) this is the wrong place for it. A different colour may sometimes be used, provided that the *tone* is not sharply different from that of ceiling or frieze. If it is, a gap is formed which breaks visual continuity and creates uneasiness. Any such change of tone, in a high room, is better introduced *below* the frieze, so that the apparent ceiling height is reduced to that level, giving horizontal rather than vertical emphasis. It can be disastrous, especially in small rooms of a rather high proportion, to remove picture rails, on whatever pretext. To do so automatically abolishes the frieze and so destroys any possibility of 'bringing down' the apparent height of the lofty ceiling. Having said this, it must also be accepted that the treatment of a tall frieze can be the trickiest of all choices to make. Anything startling is of course to be avoided, but on the other hand a plain surface completely unrelieved with texture may look forbidding. The aim should be to make the area unobtrusive by blending it gently into its surroundings, above and below. Any pictorial or decorative low-relief design in an existing frieze may reasonably be picked out, but if this is done the colours chosen, once again, must not contrast too sharply, and it may be sufficient to rely on the tracery of light reflections provided by the embossed surface.

Filling

Below the frieze and above the dado is the main area of wall, known as the 'filling'. If there is old panelling here no problem exists; and even the rather pale oak panelling widely used in the 1930's began to mellow after 20 or 30 years and to seem much more acceptable than it did when new. In some traditional bars, ceiling, wall, floor and counter-front consist entirely of painted boards, and it is remarkable how well their slightly irregular texture gives an effect both disciplined and human, tough but not rough, having

34

strength without harshness, and warmth without excessive softness. More will be said about this splendid material later when the distinctions between different 'levels' or 'moods' of bar are considered. For the moment, assuming a plastered filling, something must be done about it to dispel the bareness. Many treatments normally used for ceilings are also suitable on walls, but it is seldom enough merely to choose a warm-coloured paint. Even a large-patterned wallpaper, because the pattern is repetitive, can resolve itself into an area which appears virtually blank. Additional visual interest must be provided. This explains the popularity of mirrors, pictures and bric-à-brac, and the success of bars where the licensee has installed over the years a wealth of assorted bits and pieces to fill every available apace. It is more difficult for a designer, whose time on site is limited, to achieve such an effect from the word 'go', but at least he can make a start. If the tenant needs encouragement to carry on the process this will have to be given by brewery management. Where the licensee is himself a manager the problem is greater. Either way it is important to avoid the subtly false and contrived appearance which can result from trying to do in a few hours a job which ideally takes years of gradual, loving accretion. This is indeed a delicate subject, and it will receive further attention in the following chapter devoted to contents.

In the 1930's many large Public Bars were lined at least up to window-cill level with plain or mottled ceramic tiles of repellent appearance. I even heard of one such bar in Birmingham where ceiling, walls and floor were all of terrazzo or other impervious material so that at closing time the entire vast room could be washed down with a hose. I trust that the day has gone by for this type of thing. It offends against all proper criteria for the treatment of customers. Even if some of them do have a tendency to behave like pigs it can only encourage beastly behaviour to let them see that this is what is expected. Cleanliness and hygiene are all very well, since no-one wants the discomfort of smells or the danger of poisoning; but cleanliness can and must be obtained without a clinical or lavatorial appearance. Expanses of plain tiles, glazed brick, white, yellow or grass-green paint, stainless steel and enamel can be an insult to responsible adult drinkers. These things disperse good-fellowship and relaxation with a psychological chill like a blast of cold wind. By contrast, the visual richness of Victorian or Edwardian patterned or pictorial glazed tiles is entirely appropriate. Though they are hard they are not plain, and their sometimes rather cool colouring can be corrected by the application of warm-coloured lighting, the complete answer to any pressure which the ignorant may bring for their removal. My attitude to modern decorative tiles is Yes, fine, but they must be carefully chosen. None seem to have quite the guts of the old ones, and there is a tendency for too much white or pale-coloured background to show through the pattern – nice, maybe, in a bathroom, not so in a bar.

Architects are very fond of interior brickwork, and certainly it saves money for plaster and finishes, but the drawbacks are numerous. Being porous it quickly shows greasy patches where rubbed by fingers or clothing, and even if anyone ever thought of cleaning it the process would not be easy. Only if a really dark brick is chosen, with a dark jointing material, is brickwork normally successful, and even then it needs relief, like any other plain surface, to avoid blankness. In the country, especially in places like the Cotswolds, rough stone is popular, to a point where large areas of existing stone wall have been exposed by stripping off the plaster, but unless it is very carefully done this can appear self-conscious; and stone in urban surroundings can only look whimsically rustic. Polished granite and marble are, of course, another matter, and where they exist they should surely be kept, especially since their cost new is quite appalling.

Dado

Dadoes vary in height from less than 700 mm to more than 1700 mm. The higher ones can appear daunting, probably because we feel dwarfed – subconsciously reminded of schooldays when our eye-level was much nearer the floor. My own preference is for a dado rail at about 1150 mm which will line neatly through with the wiping strip above a counter top at the ideal 1100 mm. It is of course possible, and in modern buildings normal, to do without a dado altogether and allow the wall treatment to continue unchecked down to the floor or skirting: but for many reasons I would suggest that this should, in bars, be regarded as the exception. First, it is not practicable to hang pictures or anything else on the lower part of the wall, so that other means of avoiding visual blankness must be found. Secondly, the dado is another way of providing the horizontal emphasis we need.

Thirdly, a relatively pale or vulnerable finish such as might be suitable for the filling will not look well lower down. If it is pale in colour it will produce a visual 'gap' or 'draught' even more uncomfortable than it would be at a higher level: and if it is prone to physical damage it will soon look shabby as well. Consequently, except in the most respectable and expensive of Lounges, a dado should be both darkish and tough. In some localities it may even be right to use a flooring material such as lino to withstand the wear of feet, furniture, cleaning operations and the passage of stock trolleys before opening time. In one cattle-market pub cork tiles did very well until the adhesive failed. Not one instance comes to mind of a dado, in a pub, which would have been better omitted. Where the main wall treatment is allowed to run down between sections of seating, or is visible as a contrasting strip between the seat and back-squab of certain types of fixed seating, an uneasy sense of exposure and insecurity can result. Needless to say, all these remarks apply still more emphatically to skirtings, and the designer who paints skirtings white will suffer well-deserved hate.

Matchboarding, the virtues of which have already been mentioned, is probably the commonest of traditional materials for dadoes, and I have never yet heard a convincing excuse for doing away with it where it exists. Normally it was brush-grained – an excellent technique which we ought not to allow to die, since without it the design and redecoration of vernacular pub interiors would be virtually impossible. Some 'modern' architects, with pathetic bigotry, reject it on the ground that it imitates wood. Their strict ethical code excludes all imitations. Some craftsmen can (or could) indeed produce the most remarkable effects derived from the appearance of solid oak or mahogany boards, and I have seen external panelling skilfully painted with more knots to the square metre than could ever be grown, let alone sawn into planks! Such artistry, where it is found, can only be accepted with gratitude and admiration: but it need not be specified. The 'graining' technique is surely valid in its own right as a traditional finish, and it can be carried out with an unassuming, straight, freehand stroke which gives an interesting visual texture, and has little if any real resemblance to actual timber. It is important that the contrast in tone between undercoat and scumble should not be too great; if it is, the result will look scratchy and restless, with streaks of pale undercoat showing harshly through the warmer-coloured stain. For the same reason, too coarse a scumble brush is to be avoided. Above all, let us please eschew the pale sick-colouring once popular, and at the other extreme the sharp gingeriness of bright tan stains. Indeed it is always wise to demand fairly large trial panels or samples to ensure that the effect is right. Nor, in some places, need one despise a plain brown paint – it is better than a graining effect which has gone wrong, and sometimes it is all you require. Of course, if the wood is already polished, one would not paint it at all, though I doubt if the expense of stripping existing paint from dadoes for the sake of a 'natural' timber finish would ever be justified.

The Counter

Apart from all its other highly important functions the counter presents two more visible surfaces. The front can be regarded as part of the dado, but it suffers even greater vulnerability. Some pub customers have a great antipathy to the use of ash trays. On one counter which had been assaulted by persistent stubbing a sheet of polished copper some 500 mm deep was fixed so as to cover the burns which had been made during its first few weeks. Immediately fresh burns appeared on the polished timber *beneath* the lower edge of the copper. It seemed that the smokers were prepared to stoop, or even to climb down from their stools, for the satisfaction of destroying the polished wood. This kind of behaviour is a fact of life which must not be ignored. Strangely enough carpet, which, on the floor, would quickly be damaged by burning, survives relatively unhurt when applied to the vertical surface of a counter. This is doubtless because the cigarette end remains alight when dropped on the floor, but when it is stubbed on the counter front the fragments of ash are scattered by the pile's springiness before they can make a mark. (For this to work the carpet must contain a high proportion of wool). Other advantages of carpet (preferably patterned) as a counter front covering are that it is sympathetic to knees, and there is a wide choice of colours and patterns to give the right pub look: but it is worth remembering that in this position it will wear and lose its new appearance much less quickly than the carpet on the floor. If, therefore, one chooses the same pattern and colour of carpet for both they will not match for long. After a very few weeks the floor carpet will look shabby by contrast – an effect which will not be noticed if a different choice is made for the counter front.

Let us hope, anyway, that the bar will be so successful that whatever is used for the counter front will be totally screened from view by people for a large part of the time. In really busy pubs it is only the first-comers, morning and evening, who ever get a good look at the front of the counter: which makes it quite absurd to go in for expensive or elaborate designs involving illuminated scenes, wrought iron scrollwork, fancy rope 'cheeses', lettering or embellishments whose only purpose is to catch the client's eye in a coloured perspective.

The counter top is the most important surface in the pub. For this nothing has yet been found to improve upon wood. Being an organic substance wood is able to bring to the support of your pint and your elbow a sympathetic warmth and appropriateness totally lacking in plastic laminates. As far as mere appearance goes, some of these are fairly reasonable: it is their brittle, unyielding, synthetic quality which is out of place in a pub – more suitable, perhaps, for minerals or for milk shakes than for good beer. I flatly declare, with little fear of environmental health officials' contradiction, that it is possible to finish natural timber with a transparent melamine lacquer which is just as 'impervious' as any plastic, and yet reveals the grain of the wood: (nor does it present the exaggerated high surface gloss and treacly look of some bar topping lacquers of the past.) In general, laminates should be confined to working surfaces behind the counter, and even here dark colours must be chosen. Otherwise a clinical and chilly appearance results which is wholly at odds with convivial enjoyment, informal behaviour and a warm welcome. It is worth noting, too, that where laminate is butt-jointed even a barely visible difference in level between the two sheets will cause unsightly wear or splintering. Where trays or coins are pushed to and fro I have seen as many as half a dozen layers of microscopically thin colour exposed. Nor is this horrid material proof against cigarette burns. At the edges it is subject to splitting. The cost of eventual renewal is greater than that of sanding off and repolishing hardwood. In fact, there is much to be said for forgetting its existence. If in any particular case officialdom must be placated, one has to face the cost of falling back upon sheet metal, such as polished copper or brass. Unfortunately pewter, which for some reason seems to be specially appropriate in the 'Brewery Tap', is even more expensive. Another good material is linoleum, provided with a hardwood nosing, but a perfect joint must be made and this is not easy to guarantee. A small but important point is that on counter tops green colouring should be avoided because of its unfortunate effect on the appearance of beer.

Seating
Fixed seating presents itself to the customer's view for a good deal longer than the counter front because in most localities it is the counter which is

occupied first, while the seats fill up less quickly during the course of a session. Except at peak hours some of it will be on view, and it is therefore reasonable that the upholstery, forming a considerable part of a bar's 'enclosing surface', should be carefully chosen not only for its initial appearance but for maintenance, since anything not easily cleaned will soon look vile. Nothing is better than real hide, but its cost is likely to be prohibitive. Mohair velvet ('plush') was another splendid but expensive stuff, now virtually extinct. Its place has been taken by synthetic velvets. Moquette I always used to regard as unsuitable owing to its matt appearance. Even its uniquely hard-wearing qualities can be a drawback in any situation where a change of scene might be wanted. However, the highly respected designer Ivan Speight has made a range of moquette patterns whose character and colouring are totally 'pub', and these are worth seeking out wherever one can afford them. Leathercloth in its great variety is a most useful material for seats, and if the right colour is chosen it looks better in most pub contexts than worsted, which give no highlights and can appear dull.

There is also the question of whether or not to choose *buttoned* seating. It seems that this was pretty general in Edwardian times, and certainly its appearance is fully in keeping with interiors of that period. It also conveys a sense of luxury, and for that reason is normally out of place in a public bar. One of its advantages is the visual texture given by the buttons and pleating, which being less plain is in that way better than a straightforward squab. The glowing highlights given by a shiny material are accentuated by the undulations of the surface. This advantage is of course lost if a matt material is used, which is probably why this seldom happens and, when it does, never seems right. Another odd point is that buttoning, despite its curvilinear richness, suggests a masculine appeal, possibly because of its associations with the Gentleman's Club and the Billiards Saloon. For this reason, and other things being equal, the mood it creates is perhaps more 'Saloon Bar' than 'Lounge' – but this is a fastidious distinction in the context of seats, and I would feel free to disregard it in any individual case. I am referring, of course, to deep buttoning: to my mind the shallow variety without folding of the material is hardly worth while. A variation on this theme is vertical pleating, which I have seen used with success although for some obscure reason it is seldom encountered outside the field of motor vehicle upholstery. Whether buttons or pleats are used a practical point is that they are better confined to the back of the seating, because in a horizontal surface the cavities collect crumbs and other detritus, and aggravate the problem of cleaning.

Windows, Doors and Screens

Windows and doors must not be forgotten, and here again the chief consideration must be to avoid plainness. Victorian devices for eliminating too much view, in or out, have already been mentioned in Chapter 1 and it is a fact that the 'picture window', unrelieved by any pattern of glazing bars or decoration, normally inflicts too strong an impact of the Great Outdoors, which we have come in to escape. The only possible exception is in locations, such as riverside or hilltop pubs, where the view itself is a great attraction. (But note that at the seaside it is only the visitors, and not the natives, who will enjoy the wide horizon!) By night one has to consider the curtains. Clearly these should not be fully drawn across those windows through which potential customers are able to catch inviting glimpses of the interior: but where this does not apply it should be remembered that a wide expanse of plain curtain can be almost as offensive as an area of blank wall, and that even here it may be preferable to leave the curtains open and rely upon the subdivision of glazing for visual continuity of the enclosing surfaces. It matters little whether this consists of diamond panes, Georgian sashes or Victorian decoration – what is important is that the eye should identify and remain within the periphery of the room. Otherwise its gaze will be sucked out into the open, and its owner will lose the feeling of being protected indoors. Where there is an excess of window area it is not a bad plan to reduce it relatively cheaply by glazing part of it with silvered glass, facing inwards. In this way a window is simply converted to a framed wall mirror, and one seems to be looking through into another bar. Beware, though, of using this device in a half-glazed door. It could be a fearful let-down to push expectantly through such a door only to find oneself in a gloomy passage bound for the Gents. Apart from this, doors are only a minor problem once it is accepted that, like everything else, they should not be plain; which rules out flush doors immediately. Panelled, or possibly in country pubs ledged, braced and battened doors, are worth their cost for visual reasons alone. There is little point in fully glazed ones. An upper panel of glass is enough to let one see what is on the other side, if it is worth seeing, and if the glass can be semi-obscured by acid etching or brilliant cut work, so much the better. Indeed, it is worth while collecting such doors when old pubs are pulled down, and forming door openings and frames to fit them when alterations are made to houses of the same period.

For subdividing screens, too, patterned glass is almost essential, but I have yet to see any modern design with a tenth of the quality, in visual terms, of the work produced in Victorian and Edwardian times. I do appeal to manufacturers and designers to do what is needed, and to provide us with patterns, both standard and bespoke, as decorative as any glass bequeathed to us from the past. Meanwhile I suggest that it is an act of unspeakable vandalism to allow any such existing glazed screens, doors or windows to be destroyed when pubs are pulled down.*

Floor
By no means the least important surface enclosing a room is of course the

* For many years Ind Coope collected such 'Conservanda', and this was drawn upon by architects and designers responsible for alterations to pubs of the appropriate period, but this process had to be stopped because in 1975 it became impossible to find suitably located storage space.

40

An exceptionally splendid snob-screen

floor. Although the layout may (and should) be planned in such a way that there are no large vacant expanses, it would be optimistic to disregard the floor finish, just because, in successful bars at the busiest times, it is invisible. We must think of its appearance as well as its 'feel' to the feet. A great deal depends upon the level or 'mood' of bar, and this is referred to in Chapter 7; for the moment let us consider some of the commoner materials either surviving in old pubs or currently in use, beginning with the hardest and best and working down to the softest and least durable.

York stone flags will last as long as the building itself – probably longer. Their slight irregularity gives visual life and warmth to a bar. When worn smooth by generations of feet and kept clean with soap and water, they give a wonderful sense of permanence and continuity. Unfortunately they are being destroyed through ignorance, idleness, and a shortsighted refusal to offset their value in terms of capital and character against their cost in time and effort on the wages bill.

One of the most compulsive bars I knew was paved with blue Stafford-shire bricks.* For those not familiar with this hard, impervious engineering material it should be explained that the colour is a dark, blackish blue far removed from azure or cerulean, and it is therefore quite acceptable in relatively small areas. The bar I am referring to is in fact a beer 'cellar' some 150 mm below ground level, and in it one sits on a thrawl to drink flat-looking traditional beer from the cask: such a floor in such surroundings is entirely appropriate. Even a slightly polished concrete screed would be

* Unfortunately it has been covered (thank heaven not with carpet), with 'Rosewood' linoleum.

41

almost as good, lacking only the slight texture provided by the joints of the brickwork.

In country Tap Rooms plain red quarry tiles are still hard to beat. In the 1950's there was a vogue (for which I cannot escape some of the blame) for using heather-brown quarries instead. I now feel that their softer colour and slight mottle are insufficient compensation for their rather contrived and self-conscious appearance by comparison with the perfectly plain and un-assuming red tile. Unfortunately it is now difficult if not impossible to obtain the splendid 9×9 in tiles, and the modern 150×150 mm article lacks their more expansive scale.

Edwardian floors of rather small red, blue, buff, black and white tiles are not specifically a pub thing, but some may still be found in entrance halls and lobbies and to my mind they must always be retained; their firmness and clarity of colour and pattern is full of delight. Victorian mosaics in curvilinear patterns are also highly decorative, and surely it is a negative procedure to cover them up with materials which are plainer, or more perishable, or both. Modern mosaics have an unfortunate tendency to be fiddling and banal or flashy and ostentatious, but this remains a finish which could be used by a sensitive designer willing to take some trouble with the colour and pattern. Fully tiled floors are in any case the exception nowadays, hard materials being too often confined to a narrow strip or 'apron' less than a metre wide in front of the counter: but I suggest that those responsible may have under-estimated the willingness of the public to accept a tough, robust quality.

Partly because of this retrograde trend to softness, and partly for practical reasons, timber floors, whether blocks, strip or boards, are rapidly being done away with. Admittedly it is not always easy to keep such floors in good condition: but where this can be overcome I do beg the brewery not to take the easy way out. Any gain on the score of cleaning and maintenance may be offset by great loss of appeal. No material is more sympathetic both to foot and eye, whether polished or scrubbed. Its unique quality is all the more worthy of preservation as its rarity value increases.

In the 1950's and 60's linoleum was still the most common flooring material for rooms other than lounges, and much of it remains. It super-seded the rubber floors of the 1930's which not only ran to ghastly colour schemes of blue, white and green, but seemed cold and clammy as well, whatever the colour: a criticism that applies equally to most vinyl sheets and tiles, which enjoyed a mercifully brief vogue. The newer patterned vinyls are less offensive in this respect, but most of them are very flexible and liable to puncture or burns. Even lino can suffer from the ubiquitous fag end, but the damage is less noticeable on the marbled kinds.

With any sheet material a great deal of its visual quality depends upon the way it is cleaned. In the case of lino it is absolutely vital to see that it retains a good sheen. Do not ever use more water than will suffice to moisten a cloth or mop. This is a precept widely ignored despite continual reitera-tion by all concerned from manufacturers to brewery managers. The cleaners reckon they know better. By sloshing water about they destroy the material, but they just don't care: and to be truthful my own objection is based as much on the shocking effect too much water has on the *appearance* of lino as on the expense of renewal. Lino needs repeated application of liquid wax to feed it and to make it glow. Matt, dusty looking floors are offensive to look at even if they are chemically clean. Vacant spaces are accentuated, the warmth of light reflections is lost, and above all it is the feeling of neglect which offends against the welcome and goodheartedness which pubs ought to offer and which customers need.

Carpet, at the time of writing, is threatening to engulf like a tide all individuality in pubs and all distinctions between bars. These distinctions originated in history and are mainly a matter of mood. At one time carpet would only be used in the Lounge. So be it. A Lounge is a comparatively recent addition to the pub scene, and being derived from carpeted lounges in snooty hotels it was natural that it would require a carpet. Unfortunately the flood did not stop there. Fairly slowly at first it crept into the Smoke Room and the Saloon Bar, filling the seating alcoves, then surging across the floor to within a pace length of the counter, and finally lapping around the feet of the standing drinkers and under the foot rail until it overflowed into the cigarette trough. Now it is infiltrating even into the Public. However, for the moment let us leave these comments as it were in parenthesis and, having accepted the use of carpet as right and proper in some locations, consider its visual quality as compared with other flooring materials.

Some carpets, of course, are harder than others. It is possible, by choosing cord, or one of the popular brands with a ribbed appearance, to introduce the underfoot softness supposed (by some) to be desirable, without entirely destroying the visual toughness of a room: but here we come up against the problem of wear. Almost invariably such carpets are plain: therefore every cigarette burn, every chewing-gum splodge, will show up like a cow pat in a field. Pattern, in pub carpet, is almost a *sine qua non*: which inevitably leads to the use of the more expensive Wilton body carpet available in such variety of pattern that we are faced with an *embarras de choix*. It would hardly be practicable to explore the entire range. Nevertheless, I throw out a few hints:

1. The larger the pattern the more effective will be the camouflage in any unavoidably blank area.
2. Geometric patterns give a stronger effect, more appropriate to pubs than 'floral arrangements', unless the latter are very much stylised rather than naturalistic.
3. Modern geometric patterns can be laid without offence in many old rooms, but there are a few particular types of room such as the Snug where only traditional Turkey red seems right.
4. Too many colours can be restless, unsettling, crude and ostentatious, which suggests that multi-colour Axminsters are less likely to be successful.

43

However, when all has been said about carpet, there is in the 1980's a glimmer of hope that we shall be able to stem the flood, if only on grounds of cost. A square metre of pub floor must sell a lot more beer in a year to pay for itself if it is carpeted than if it is not!

Colour and Texture

Colour, in fact, although it has hardly been mentioned till now, has a most important effect psychologically, and though it is not of course confined to surfaces, it is from these that it provides its greatest impact. I have already said that to give a sense of *seclusion* it is necessary for all surfaces to be relieved with pattern or with visual incident of some kind. It is the choice of colour which can contribute to the feeling of *welcome*. The standard description of a welcome is 'warm', from which it follows that 'warm' colours must predominate in any scheme intended to convey a welcome.

The colours most widely accepted as warm, probably because of their close association with fire, are those which contain some red. Pale blues, greens and most greys, on the other hand, suggest cold water and ice, and their widespread use must therefore be rejected as unwelcoming. They must be restricted to quite small areas which can accentuate by contrast the effect of the predominantly warm colour scheme. A bar billiards table, for instance, or a few vivid green lampshades, can introduce a note of liveliness without in any way detracting from the warmth of a mellow interior.

It is helpful to remember that all colours, including those on the cold side of the colour circle, appear warmer in their darker tones, and conversely warm colours in their lighter tones give a cooler effect. For this reason, when some cool colours are chosen, it is best to use them in darker tones, whilst warm colours need not be so dark. Beware, though, the use of too much *pink*, which is undeniably a pale tone of red, but which is undesirable because of its nursery and boudoir associations. Bottle green, however, being almost black, is by no means out of place. Indeed it is not a bad guide to say that all colours associated with drinks, from Burgundy or Guinness to pale ale, are good colours for drinking places, with the possible exception of the greener types of 'white' wine. Even the colours of Creme-de-Menthe or of Blue Bols can be used in their appropriate tiny proportions as accents or sharp contrasts to enliven the scene.

It is also true that the warm, glowing colours of the fireside have still a strong association with hospitality. We welcome friends and strangers to our 'hearth and home'. Its colours, therefore, are perfect in pubs, and this includes the wonderfully rich, glossy colour of clean coal – ("an agreeable, dark hue, which the satirical call 'black'" – RLS). Many people are afraid of black, thinking that it must be funereal. If it is matt this may be true, but a glossy surface, whatever its hue, will reflect every light and colour which is there to be reflected; this means that its effect will very largely depend upon what is provided in the rest of the room. A dark glossy surface will contribute depth and mellowness in a warm environment, and even a white surface, if it is glossy, will in the same context appear less offensive than if it were matt. The reasons for avoiding a predominance of matt surfaces were discussed earlier, but it should be said that this does not imply the need for a high, hard, superficial gloss on everything. This is, indeed, the only right condition of some materials, such as glass and certain polished metals, but for others, such as leather and timber, a depth or richness of patina is often the more natural finish, and paint may be chosen or mixed to give a considerable variation of degrees of lustre. The object is to ensure, by a number of accurate decisions, that the texture of the whole design should combine with appropriate colour and carefully arranged lighting to give the warm glow of a welcoming appearance. To the extent that the proper reflective qualities are lacking this effect will be lost. For example, in some interiors, especially those based on the 'olde worlde' formula, high gloss paintwork is out of place except for minor detail and trim (e.g. window frames). This type of treatment presupposes a wealth of well-polished dark oak furniture, and of copper and brass, which themselves fulfil the need for reflective surfaces, so that nothing is more suitable as a background than the traditional whitish or pale cream walls, with no higher a finish than egg-shell, crossed and recrossed with an intersecting pattern of structural timbers.

A country alehouse was once described in these terms: ". . . the wood-work of the high-backed settles, no less than the surface of the roughly plastered walls, indicate a finish by contact, unnoticed and unintentional." We cannot, without the passage of time, achieve this splendid ideal in every bar; and heaven forbid that we should descend to faking new surfaces to look old: but we can choose materials which are natural, sympathetic and warm, rather than harsh, synthetic and brittle, thus providing the conditions in which this comfortable appearance can grow. Such materials are durable and timeless in character. Given proper care they will improve with age, and contribute to the drinking scene that mellowness and permanence which is so important a component of the 'essence of pub'.

5 Pub Contents

Everything a bar contains is part of its contents. It should not be necessary to state this truism, but far too many excellent pubs are visually marred because it seems that nobody has made it his business to *look*, in order to ensure that *nothing* is allowed to infiltrate which sticks out like the proverbial sore thumb. Either they do look, and simply cannot discriminate, or more probably, there are too many cooks. Normally the designer is not allowed to finish his job. When he has done his best the place is invaded by beer dispense fitters, sound engineers, marketing men, the licensee's wife. One-armed bandits, advertisement cards, and a mass of smelly flowers in deformed vases intrude into the scene. Grey cable is draped from beam to beam, and display shelves designed to carry a multitude of colourful, gleaming bottles are filled instead with cans which for all they contribute to the pub character might as well contain milk.

Contents, of course, are bound to include people, and first among the people present in any pub is the licensee himself. When The Champion, London W.1, was re-opened it was said that the architects, John and Sylvia Reid, had even specified the couple who took over as Guv'nor and Missus, but few designers can hope to be granted such privilege. Appointments of this kind are the job of the brewery manager or director, whose choice is inevitably based on criteria other than candidates' aesthetic appeal, or their discrimination of things visual. Unfortunately, men like David Kitching of the Crown and Greyhound, Dulwich, Pat Murray late of the Brown Bear, Stepney, and George Olman of the Double Diamond, Rotterdam, are few and far between. The job of looking and enhancing is therefore left to the same brewery officials. Again, some are able and some not. I trust that the latter group may benefit from reading this book.

It is even possible to control to some extent the type of customer using a bar. Some licensees take great pains, with varying degrees of subtlety, to deter whole sections of the population. They are lucky to be able to do so. Clearly they are wise to exclude from their general welcome all thugs, villains and vandals. However, when they choose to reject anyone who wears no tie, or his hair long, or who speaks with a 'posh' accent, the pub at once becomes something less than a pub. It no longer fits the description given by Leslie Forse, formerly editor of *The Morning Advertiser*, as "... the haunt of the common man ... the citizen who whatever his rank or position meets other citizens as equals at the bar." What, then, can a guv'nor do when he feels, possibly quite correctly, that the look of his lounge is adversely affected by a thirsty horde of strapping young fellows in dirty boots, shirts open to the waist and sleeves rolled up to display hairy tummies and tattooed arms. The answer is that they are probably only there because there is no appropriate bar in the pub where they would not look (and feel) out of place. Similarly, a good business men's Smoke Room or Saloon Bar invaded by a gaggle of young ladies becomes totally useless for its specialized trade; and the business men themselves would undesirably transform the look of a country tap room or a dock-side Vaults. These important distinctions will be studied in detail later. I mention them now to make the point referred to in my second Principle of Pubness given on page 23. Contents can be chosen to make different sorts of people feel 'at home': but having said this, the test of every article placed in a bar, from the chairs and tables to the smallest liqueur glass, from the ashtrays to the barman's pale blue cardigan and Madam's carpet slippers, is whether it enhances or detracts from the scene as designed for social drinking.

Old Pub Furniture

Nowadays furniture proper to pubs is not easy to find. In earlier times tables, settles, benches and stools were made which, whether or not they were purposely designed for use in pubs, were eminently suitable. Happily, much of this stuff remains, and one has only to look at it carefully to see that it has two common characteristics – elegance and strength. Despite its elegance it is (and looks) strong. Despite its strength its form is full of subtle delight in proportion and detail. At the time it was made, these two qualities, elegance and strength, were clearly not considered to be mutually exclusive. Why should they be? It is, however, sadly evident that this is no longer the case. Furniture strong enough for pub use tends to be ill-proportioned, crude and clumsy: conversely, the better looking articles are either delicate and flimsy, grossly expensive, or made of 'new' materials which are unsympathetic in appearance. Some metal pieces may in fact be durable and tough, but they still look spindly, thin and vulnerable. For this reason alone they are unacceptable in the robust context of a drinking room. It makes no sense at all, therefore, in economic or visual terms, to throw out the old furniture simply in order to spend money on new.

Of traditional pub components the oldest survivor is probably the high-backed settle, normally curved on plan, and placed end-on to one side of the tap room fire-place in such a way that the people remote from the wall are brought forward just sufficiently to get a glimpse of the fire. The gentle curve also has the effect of turning the occupants slightly inwards – their lines of vision converge at a point well within the room, and those at the

The rectangular cast-iron table is called (for some reason unknown to the author) the Lion Table. Note the moulded edge to the top and especially the slightly radiused corners

What could be more appropriate for a Tap Room than this fine traditional chair. Such pieces, produced by the work of successive generations of sensitive craftsmen, cannot easily be improved upon

Strong and elegant bar stools such as these are well worth collecting and renovating. Usually only the foot rails require renewal after decades of hard use: but when inserting new rails do not use modern adhesives, which may prevent a further renewal after another fifty or a hundred years!

extreme ends can see each other's faces without the discomfort of edging forward and sideways on to one ham, as they would have to do if seated on a straight bench. Apart from the functional aspect of this companionable arrangement, both the curved back and the shaped ends of the settle have an elegance and inevitability which cannot fail to delight the eye. Only really

The Saloon Bar or Smoke Room padded bench seat has a perfection of its own

traditional things can have such perfection. Long ago, when young and inexperienced, I made the mistake of trying to improve on the curve of the shaped settle-end to bring it 'up-to-date' in terms of 'modern' design. Others have tried to reproduce or copy the traditional shape without success, apparently because they have not taken the trouble to look at an authentic original. As Frank Bradbeer pointed out to me, the curve is extremely flat at the top, not bulbous; and the arm rest is almost an S-bend. Bogus reproductions are invariably, by comparison, crude and ill-formed. Surely there can be no harm in copying exactly a shape which has been arrived at by trial and error through the centuries by generation after generation of sensitive craftsmen.

Some of the more luxurious Victorian and Edwardian built-in seating was also made in curves, and it is always delightful. Loose benches of the type normally used in less exalted bars came in straight pieces of various lengths, but they were faultlessly designed and beautifully detailed. The turned front legs, very slightly raked padded back and carved arms all fit smoothly together and give an excellent drinking posture. Even the public bar version made partly of plywood (known as tram seating) was a highly decorative piece of furniture, the moulded seat and back ergonomically shaped to fit the human form, and relieved with geometrical patterns of perforations. It is stupid to fit padding to these fine old seats to make them more comfortable – it has, in fact, the reverse effect, because the padding

50

interrupts the smoothly moulded shape, and the seat and back no longer support the body from the crook of the knee to the shoulder blade as was intended – and achieved – by the designer.

If, for some reason (and I cannot think of a good one) it is desired to 'lush up' the look of a tram seat, it is possible to do so without spoiling the shape, by applying a fabric such as moquette, *without* padding. Thus the curve of the seat and back is virtually unchanged, and the comfort remains.

Tall bar stools were designed most ingeniously to fit the human backside, the seats being carved from solid timber. My own rotund base is well above average size, but the tolerance is sufficient even for me, and I believe that only the most cadaverous characters with protruding bones could justly complain of discomfort. Nevertheless some nincompoops have in the past, for reasons best known to themselves, even applied padding to these elegant stools, destroying their visual quality and the comfort of their shape at one fell stroke. Let us, please, have an end to this wanton and wasteful vandalism! All such furniture deserves to be carefully restored, the joints reglued, the worn rails replaced, the timber cleaned and wax-polished, and the upholstery (where it exists) properly remade, It is less expensive in the long run to restore something old than to buy something cheap.

The three-legged cast-iron table (commonly called the Britannia) is at least safe from extinction, at any rate for the time being. Its fabulous qualities have ensured a continuing demand to the point where quite adequate reproductions are being made from new moulds. It has never been improved upon for pub use, being strong enough to resist all but the most deliberate impact damage, and at the same time as elegant as only an article consisting almost entirely of curves could be. The double curve of the leg is an object lesson in solid geometry, and as epoch making in its way as the famous pendentives of Santa Sophia. One word of warning. When tops are relaced please, please use solid timber, or lino with a timber nosing, or marble – not laminate, which is totally wrong. Please, also, insist that the edge is moulded. A square-section top looks most uneasy in the context of the curved elevations and circular plan. Another little tip is that the cast-iron frame can look extremely well if sand-blasted to remove all the paint, and then varnished. The decorative work can still, if you wish, be picked out in gilt. In some types of room to paint the whole frame gilt can also look right, but in my opinion the use of 'fancy' colours such as red, blue or orange on these tables is out of place.

Rectangular cast-iron tables of the same period share many, though not all, of the same qualities, and these are also worth preserving. Some have tops not more then 250 mm wide, with semi-circular ends – quite adequate for the support of a few pints. Being highly economical of floor space these tables are ideal in long narrow bars where the passage between counter and wall is restricted.

Another traditional table much used in old pubs is appropriately enough the Victorian 'kitchen table', originally placed in public bars with their kitchen tradition. This is often disdained, but to my mind, if provided with a polished hardwood top having the original shape and moulding it is worthy of use in any part of the house. The turned legs are sturdy without looking heavy or crude, the rail in the best examples has a little quirk which very subtly lightens its appearance, and the radiused corners of the top allow one to edge in and out of one's seat without danger of groin injury.

Counters and backfittings, even more than loose furniture, are very often worth keeping, especially the Victorian ones. It is sometimes necessary in days of less numerous staff, to reduce the extent of the service area, which is bound to involve a corresponding reduction in the length and possibly a complete rearrangement of the counters. Fortunately the backfittings, which are likely to contain virtually irreplaceable decorative mirrors with carved, turned and moulded woodwork, are generally shorter, so that it may be possible to keep them *in situ*, or move them to another location within the building. In any case it is unthinkable that one should permit destruction of any such work, and if they cannot be re-used in the same pub they could perhaps be stored and placed in another when alterations are done. At the very least, all the brilliant-cut and french-embossed mirrors should surely be preserved. In the case of counters it is normally only the panelled fronts which can be saved, but it is sad to see the fine curved pewter work in undercounters replaced by laminate having no comparable craftsmanship or character. Needless to say, where a counter is replanned and a new top has to be fitted it ought to be provided with the appropriate generously moulded hardwood nosing, and even if cost forbids the use of solid timber for the whole top, linoleum is a preferable finish to any plastic laminate in such a context.

One of the most delightful of all pub fixtures is the one which is, in fact, peculiar to the pub – the magnificent 'snob-screen'. This was a Victorian invention consisting of a polished mahogany structure fixed to the counter top and containing small panes of decorative glass in centre-pivoted timber frames. This allowed the 'snobs' in the Saloon Bar to be served and at the same time to cut themselves off from the direct scrutiny of the lower orders – perhaps their own servants or employees – in the Public Bar. It is certainly true that this requirement has far less importance, if indeed it has any, in the second half of the 20th century. Worse still, being designed as a barrier, the snob-screen can be rightly criticized for having the undesirable effect of cutting off the customers from those whose job it is to offer a welcome and to serve them with drinks. No doubt this is almost enough to explain its virtual disappearance. Nonetheless, one can only deplore the complete loss of any object so decorative and splendid. What is quite unforgivable is that snob-screens should be removed on this or any other pretext, only to be replaced, either by a suspended canopy producing the 'hole-in-the-wall' or slot effect, (see Chapter 3 Spatial Qualities), or by a fancy pot rack of imitation wrought iron, either of which gives even more offensive separation, and looks idiotically out of place into the bargain. In my view the beauty of Victorian snob-screens is enough to compensate for quite a lot of inconvenience or discomfort. At all events, even if it is decided that the time has come for them to be removed from any particular bar, surely it is possible to re-instate them as permanent screens between alcoves, or in some other situation where their visual splendour can still be enjoyed.

New Pub Furniture

However, when all is said and done about old fittings and furniture in pubs, and whatever efforts are made to keep them in use, it has to be conceded that in quantity they cannot be sufficient for our present-day needs. In almost all cases it is necessary to buy or to build something new, and one is forced to overcome the difficulty I have described. In trying to do so, we shall certainly fail unless we keep in mind the two criteria, elegance and strength, which are still requirements in any age. More or less successful attempts have indeed been made, by Ray Carter in the 1950's and later by Michael Jacks, to design modern furniture which can satisfactorily be used in pubs. Many of their pieces are still in use at the time of writing: but they were exclusive to Allied Breweries. Others have produced copies, or fallen back onto the standard ranges of the big bar-fitting firms, which were pretty unsightly, or cheap café furniture which looked even worse. A rash of pink, grey, blue, buff linette and yellow laminate ruined the visual quality of too many bars. Later, some firms produced tables, chairs and stools which, if not exactly reproductions, at any rate had a strong element of reminiscence. These are less offensive, though rather costly. We need a talented designer to re-interpret and revive the tradition for modern methods of production.

When choosing furniture it is of course necessary to bear in mind not only its appearance but its dimensions. Space is not to be squandered. A table for drinking need only be large enough to support half a dozen pints and an ash tray. Dominoes need a little more space, and players object to a circular table. Full-scale meals, too, demand special provision, but where the level of catering is simple pub grub any table big enough for drinking is normally adequate for one's plate and fork as well. People in pubs expect to put up with a certain degree of restriction of movement, and seem quite content to pull in their elbows. Chairs should also be limited in size, and it is my belief that where there is plenty of fixed seating only small stools need be provided. At all events the area occupied by an average bar chair need not exceed about $0.25m^2$. In the more expensive type of lounge it is reasonable to be a little more generous, but even here it is worth remembering that the floor space occupied by a seated customer is greatly increased if he cannot get his legs under the table. This means that low tables of the type favoured in hotel coffee lounges are very extravagant, and should never be chosen without a conscious decision that, for whatever reason, no other sort will do. The additional licensed area gained by a costly structural alteration can be entirely negatived by the choice of such furniture. No more people are accommodated than before the room is extended. In such circumstances not only are the customers restricted in number – they are more widely separated from each other, which is less companionable and makes conversation more difficult. Voices are then raised and we have a noise problem as well. Reclining chairs, too, are ill-adapted for conversation in any room where the sound level is high, as it is bound to be at peak trading times even without music. The normal attitude of a seated drinker (left elbow on table, right hand on glass, trunk and head inclined slightly forward to speak or listen) suggests that if a seat back is needed at all it should be vertical, with a bulge for lumbar support. The part of the chairback more than 750–800 mm above floor level is nearly superfluous. I am assuming a standard seat height of 450 mm, because anything lower demands the provision of waiter service. The greater the effort needed to get up and down the fewer the rounds that will be taken.

People who choose to drink at the counter – 'perpendicular drinking' it used to be called – do so for three main reasons: contact with the guv'nor and staff, the chance of congenial encounter, and proximity to the source of supply. In most bars it is therefore essential to provide tall stools so that we who carry 'excess' weight, and other idle customers, may relieve their feet of the load. Some licensees prefer to deny this facility to their patrons, claiming that others in the room cannot get served: but this is an argument which in my view should be rejected. All that is needed is good bar manners to let the thirsty edge through. If there is one stool only at the counter, and it is occupied, I am content to stay for another half in the hope to getting it, but if there is none I will drink up and depart. One stool is therefore the minimum, but I believe that even in a small room with a counter only 2m long there is room for two, leaving a space between for service. In longer bars it is probably better to leave two thirds of the length without stools. In Holland, where the entire counter is lined with stools, at 600 mm centres, fixed to the floor, waiter service has to be provided, and the prices of drinks reflect the unnecessary wages involved.

A well-designed counter stool top is square or rectangular rather than circular: the height of the stool is 750–800 mm, and robust rails are provided for the feet at two different heights. Only in very smart cocktail bars or at snack counters are back-rests sometimes provided, and there are people who find a stool with a back less comfortable than one without. Padding and upholstery nearly always suffer from deliberate and accidental damage, and I doubt very much if the demand for these really comes from the customers. Ray Carter designed a stool for public bars entirely of timber, with a dished top of two-inch thick laminations (this was before metrication) bolted together, and a padded version for saloon bars: but a modified all-timber design was specially made for the cocktail bar of a four-star hotel, and this became popular. The seat was a good deal bigger, and if one accepts the implication that the up-market customers are discriminating enough to appreciate the sophistication of a wooden stool, it is hard to reject the corollary, that they are also much bigger built!

Whatever furniture is chosen, it is worth while seeing that it is well arranged in the room, The regimentation of chairs and tables in long, straight rows may be all right for a cafeteria, but the rigid appearance is surely inappropriate in a place intended for social drinking. An informal

This counter in a Cardiff bar is nearly 20 metres long

layout will better encourage relaxation and good fellowship. A bit of higgledy-piggledy is all to the good.

In many, and especially in new pubs, a serious shortcoming is that all the furniture is of a uniform pattern, manufactured, delivered and installed at the same time. This cannot help but give an institutionalised appearance. It helps if you can introduce a few odd pieces of individual character, not just mixed in with the rest so as to give an accidental, untidy look, but placed apart as something which the licensee is proud to possess.

Collections

Similarly, licensees' collections of things not only help the look of the place by filling in offensive areas of blank wall space: they also add to the sense of being made welcome in somebody's home, because they reflect the personal taste or hobby of the man who is our host. Almost anything can be collected. Perhaps the most famous example is the Bear at Oxford, where glass fronted cabinets full of ties cover every available piece of wall. Matchboxes, toy cars, fire-arms, butterflies – there are few portable items which have not, at one time or another, been used to adorn a bar. I remember a place in Mansfield where there were so many clocks that the susurration of their ticking could be heard across the entrance hall at opening time. A collection of road signs in a Hackney pub was less successful in a decorative sense, but at least it was a try. For preference, whatever is chosen ought to be the licensee's genuine interest, and whatever it is it must not be visually overwhelming. A gimmick

55

should not be allowed to reach the point where it intimidates the customers and overshadows the occupation of social drinking.

It is, of course, quite possible to accumulate articles of so many different sorts that they have little or nothing in common with each other except that they are all in one room. This is hardly a serious collection, but it can still perform the function of filling in spaces which would otherwise be bare. A balance must be kept between disinterest and self-consciousness. Certainly, to leave the walls blank suggests that the customer is regarded by the management with no more respect or consideration than a traveller will find in a station waiting room. On the other hand, theme pubs (like the Printer's Devil when it was new) can become tedious with rows of showcases, the exhibits neatly docketed and labelled. Again, this is because they have become more like a museum – an institution – rather than a welcoming, friendly and informal pub.

Bric-à-Brac

By far the most common choice of bric-à-brac is the olde worlde, agricultural or stable-yard theme. This has penetrated deep into the town, and can even be found in pubs with such unlikely names as The Saracen's Head or The Hope and Anchor. Similarly, nautical impedimenta crop up in The Bull! Possibly the underlying reason for the popularity of these two themes is that each of them reminds us of the timeless elements, old Mother Earth and the changeless sea, in some sort compensating for the fact that in our civilisation most of us are amputated from these basic things: in other words, there may be some connection here with the fifth pub principle, continuity. Indeed, at one time these two formulae, the rustic and the nautical, seldom failed. Rooms were small and the articles remained in scale. From horse brasses and pewter tankards through warming pans and copper measures to binnacles and ship's lanterns, the bits and pieces seemed to have some connection with the place as a tavern, or at least as a travellers' inn. The areas of wall were never enormous and they were easily filled. Warm light was reflected from polished metal, and sparkled amidst the mellow brown of the surroundings. All was unassuming, domestic and comforting. However, when the attempt was make to apply this treatment to rooms as big as barns, inevitably it failed. Despite the use of larger and larger pieces, horse collars, cart-wheels, anchors and capstans, even whole vehicles hung from the roof, or thirty-foot sections of ship's mast, not only did the whole thing get out of hand but vacant white areas of wall persisted in between the gimmickry, and the visual objective was not achieved. Worse, the general effect of such exaggerated treatment is crassly absurd, insincere, ostentatious, sadly inappropriate to the business in hand. Social drinking is never solemn: but if anyone supposes that it is not serious, he is wide of the mark.

Curtains

Another furnishing component which is commonly overdone, less obtrusive but possibly more insidious, is the excessive provision of curtains. Too much drapery can introduce a note of softness and gentility. A rational approach is surely needed, to avoid not only this unsuitable effect, but also a lot of needless expense.

Curtains, in a home, have four main functions: to give privacy, and to give protection against light, heat or cold from outside. In a pub the first role is less important, though it is true to say that most pub customers do prefer not to be stared at by passers by. On the other hand, as I have suggested earlier when considering the effect of windows on space, and looking at curtains as surfaces, there are good reasons for not filling the whole of every window with drapes. To do so cuts off the people outside from inviting glimpses of the interior, and at the same time it denies customers the subtle satisfaction of keeping a tenuous link with the outside world. Consequently, enough privacy is given if the view from the street is screened up to the standing eye-level of pedestrians, and even this need not apply if the pub is set well back from the road. This provision can be made by decorative obscured glass, or by short curtains hung from a transome or rail.

Something more is needed to keep out the rays of the sun when they are nearly horizontal, but this problem mainly arises in the case of windows facing west. The sun is often high enough by morning opening time to avoid discomfort in bars facing east or south-east, especially in towns. Sky glare from other quarters can best be dealt with by means of deep pelmets, stained glass in the upper panes, roller blinds, or Dutch blinds externally. All these have minor disadvantages, and the choice must be made on the merits of each case; but it is safe to say that in the great majority of bars it is an extravagance to hang curtains for the full width and height of the windows. If curtains are needed in a Lounge or Smoke Room for their softening effect or for any other visual reason, dress curtains (which cannot be drawn across the glass) will be quite adequate for the purpose, and have the added advantage that they are much less costly to install, to clean and to replace.

Net or muslin curtains are another way of screening, but unless they are very carefully organised a note of excessive femininity seems to creep in. My own strong inclination is to eschew them; but it must be admitted that occasionally one sees in a certain type of small, tenanted, back-street, family-trade pub a concoction of net curtain so elaborate, so lovingly and decoratively fashioned, that the thing becomes an *objet d'art* in its own right. No one in his right mind is likely to complain about that.

Only when the heating system is defective, the bar empty, and the window area much too large anyway, should keeping out the cold be a function of pub curtains. For the odd occasion when there is a blizzard or hailstorm it is hardly worth the cost of installing full curtains, but if there are roller blinds they could be used. To prevent their presenting an offensive blank space to the eye they could be made of decorative fabric, or stencilled pattern could be applied. In any case, I am by no means sure that wintry

57

weather does not accentuate rather than detract from one's satisfaction and enjoyment in the warmth of the bar.

Fireplaces

Although this is not the place to make any further mention of heating systems, which ought to be taken for granted, perhaps it is a convenient moment to consider the fireplace, not as a source of heat but as an item in the list of contents. It does seem that, despite the powerful symbolism of the welcoming hearth, an open fire is no longer essential in most bars. There was a time not so very long ago when such a statement would have sounded like heresy. Is not the fireplace the focal point of the room? Until the advent of television this was certainly true of domestic sitting rooms, and heaven forbid that the TV should ever become the focal point of a bar! However, the true focus of attention in any good bar is surely the point of supply, with it s backdrop of gleaming bottles in the backfitting display. I suggest that no one who has passed a winter evening contentedly in a crowded bar, without noticing that the fireplace was non-existent, can afterwards maintain that it is necessary to have one. For all that, I hope my words will not be taken as a pretext for eliminating any fireplace where the space is available, and where the staff are able and willing to cope with the work involved, especially if the hearth and surround form an essential part of the room's architectural character.

Display

Because, as I have said, it is not in the shopkeeper's interest that his customers should hang about taking up space once their shopping is done, his display is designed to sell as directly, crudely and quickly as can be contrived. In a pub it is different. Subject to your good behaviour, you are welcome to stay and be served until the law decrees otherwise. This fairly obvious fact seems never to have dawned upon the average marketing man, who tries to apply to the relatively static drinking situation the sort of brash, instant appeal which, in the supermarket, is meant to stop a housewife in full cry. In a bar, the shelves are not competing for our attention as we move past: they form instead a focal point and a background to us as we sit or stand. It follows that they must be more subtle than strident; and offer contentment rather than cacophony. In any case, how relevant is any 'point-of-sale' material in a bar? How many people look at the shelves to decide what to drink? Two or three at the most, perhaps, in an evening, and they are people unused to pubs, wasting the barman's time while they debate the relative merits of Perry or Pernod. At best a casual caller may look round in order to identify the brewer, so as to order by its brand name the house pale ale. The rest of us know already what is there to be had. Advertisements are of supreme irrelevance. But we will stay the longer and no doubt drink an extra pint or two of what we came in for, if the cockles of our hearts are warmed by a vision of gleaming bottles, exotic in variety, rich with glowing colour and extravagant in plenty. This can best be organised without cards or cans. A lot depends upon lighting, and this I will examine in Chapter 6: for the moment, suffice it to suggest that your backfitting will sell nothing directly. It will not help sales of a particular product: but it may well have a momentous effect upon trade in general by inducing in the customer a mellow and generous mood. Conversely, of course, if the shop-window-dressers get their way, it may even be counter-productive.

One sometimes hears brewery managers complain about a licensee's use of a backfitting for the display of decorative oddments which are not for sale – dolls, fancy bottles, pewter tankards, heraldic shields, plastic hop-vines. To my mind, they are being too meticulously commercial. The effect of such things depends entirely on the way they are arranged, and if they contribute to a feeling of warmth and richness they can do no sort of harm. Another common complaint is about the number of glasses on display shelves, and I agree that this can be overdone. It is convenient to have spirits glasses near the optics, but beer glasses are probably better under the counter. In certain sorts of country pub glass and metal tankards are often hung by their handles from the low ceiling with good effect (but beware the Enviromental Health Officer . . .). I can see little real objection to a display of vulgar postcards, received from regulars on holiday, as long as they are not too ancient and flyblown. More offensive than any of these things is a mass of cigarette packets, while cigarette dispensing machines can be a gross intrusion, whether they are behind the counter or fixed to a bar wall. I tend to resent, too, the way some licensees arrange stacks of inappropriate merchandise such as chocolate and chewing gum, which make the place look like a sweet-shop. Aspirins, breath-sweeteners, peanuts and crisps are more germane to the licensed trade, but a great deal more attention deserves to be paid to the way they are shown, to avoid a feeling of tattiness, restlessness and agitation. Point-of-sale material, too, can look a mess. Drip mats and counter towels can be overdone, especially if they are old and soiled. Rubber or plastic mats attract and retain moisture which quickly destroys the polish on the counter. I suppose that nobody can seriously object to a couple of collecting boxes or Christmas stockings for charitable objects, but again, moderation is needed. Surely the traditional heap of coins or a large bottle half full of them look better, and may be more effective as well. The principle to remember when considering any of these minor contents of a bar is, at any rate, quite clear. A pub is not a shop, and if it looks like one the customers may well react unfavourably.

Clocks

A clock is a very important piece of furniture in a bar, because of Permitted Hours. It is easier for the licensee to point to a clock on the wall than to the watch on his wrist. Normally clocks in pubs, for obvious reasons, are ten minutes fast, more or less. I will never forget the case of the White Lion Bars, Coventry, where all the clocks were controlled by a master clock in the Hotel Leofric lounge, which was itself activated (or so we were told) by a series of impulses transmitted direct from the Greenwich observatory. It was therefore impossible for them to be wrong. This caused poor Steve Lewis, the manager, a good deal of trouble. One morning he came to me wringing his hands. Please, please, could we have the clocks put on the traditional ten minutes, because last night a large Irish labouring man had disputed the point with him, not believing that a pub clock could be right. "He nearly filled me in", said Steve plaintively. Later I heard the same story from another source. "You should have seen Steve at closing time last night", said my friend. "Here was this great Irishman arguing the toss, and next minute he found himself out in the street, pint and all!" The amusing part of this occurrence was that dear old Steve affected a rather mincing mode of speech, and thereby gave to many a totally deceptive impression of effeminacy.

All honest clocks have circular faces, because the hands go *round*. Square or rectangular clocks are a contradiction in terms. Digital clocks may be all very well in a railway terminus, but will not, I hope, ever be used in bars. There was, in fact, one that I knew in the Crown, Clerkenwell, where several dozen delightful old clocks provided the pub theme, and gave each the time in a different part of the world. The digital clock was the only one registering GMT or BST as the case may be. This, I felt, was just about acceptable.

A bar clock deserves a good quality case. Metal cases of 'factory-type' clocks give a cheap and sub-standard appearance. Bar clocks should also be generous in proportions, and unless the room is very small, 25 mm diameter is the minimum acceptable size: 30 mm is better and 35 mm better still. A possible exception may be nautical clocks in bars with a nautical gimmick, simply because it is hard to find one bigger than 20 mm. Normally, on any kind of clock, Roman figures give a better effect than Arabic.

No better clock has ever been made for use in bars than the standard 19th-century mahogany-cased pendulum clock. 'Act of Parliament' clocks are, of course, entirely splendid, but they have become collectors' pieces, and in any case are far to big for the average bar.

Grandfather clocks can be a confounded nuisance in congested bars, and take up a lot of useful floor space; but in a certain kind of country pub such a venerable timepiece can, oddly enough, contribute a sense of time-lessness! Perhaps it is because of its unhurried gait, and the feeling of antiquity which it exudes. Other sorts of domestic clock, including the once popular sun-ray type, are normally too small and mean for use in a pub.

Potshelves

I have given warning of the ill effect of canopies arranged in such a way that the upstand follows the counter line in the same vertical plane as the counter front. Potshelves must be carefully handled to avoid a similar effect. A continuous potshelf, whether suspended from above or supported on stan-dards, makes a sort of cage in which the bar staff appear to have been imprisoned, reducing their status in our eyes, and forming a division between them and us. Why is it that so many new tenant licensees no sooner take up their position behind the counter than they set up an insistent demand for a potshelf? I do not believe it is anything to do with the storage of glasses, as they always claim. I think they do it because of timidity. No doubt subconsciously, they feel the need of protection from the public. But to thrust the customers away in this manner, to exclude them from what then becomes an inner sanctum, is rather unfriendly. I wish they could see how absurd they look, cowering behind their often quite unnecessary defensive barricade.

Worst of all potshelves is the bent-iron article, with its bogus-rustic, sentimental, gnomes'-whimsical look. Once only have I seen a wrought iron potshelf which did not detract from the look of the bar: at the famous Crown and Greyhound at Dulwich. Because of the subdued lighting it is barely visible, and it serves mainly as support for some excellent Venetian glass arranged upon it for decorative effect. Normally, the rusticity of the standard iron potshelf looks out of place in the town, while in the country its cheapness and falseness is accentuated. It is not that there is anything wrong with the material itself – it is the way it is frilled and twisted about, the banal design, which offends. Painted gilt, the things look ghastlier still.

Beer Pump Handles

Beer pump handles are among the few pub components which seldom if ever appear elsewhere. For this reason alone they are valuable *signals*; they contribute powerfully to the recognisability of a pub interior, a fact which is attested by their use in humorous cartoons, along with the dartboard, to indicate the place in which the scene of a jest is set. Beside this, they have a sculptural strength and elegance which, even regarded as abstract form, gives delight. The traditional shape is composed entirely of curved lines and surfaces. In the 20's and 30's a mistaken effort was made to 'modernise' their appearance, by using a cylindrical shaft. A cylinder, of course, presents two straight lines to the eye, and this immediately detracts from the beauty of the artefacts. Not content with this solecism, the modernisers went farther and smoothed out the strongly moulded base into a truncated cone, again substituting a straight-sided object for the satisfying curves of the original form.

Worse still was to come with the onset of keg beer and pressure service. Beer pumps were banished and their place taken by a squalid row of deformed and strident boxes, competing with each other for our attention, and transforming a splendid piece of Victorian engineering into a visual slum. It seemed that no excess of tasteless innovation was enough to satisfy the marketing men. The only brewery departments not consulted about the production of these messy intruders were the architects'; consequently the word 'design' as applied to these things is a sour joke.

One of the benefits conferred by the Trad Beer Revival of the 1970's was the restoration of beer pumps to the scene in the bar. Only a few years before many thousands of installations had been torn out and sold for scrap at 7s. 6d. a pull (37½p). The brewers paid dearly for their lack of foresight.

61

Footrails

Even for footrails wrought iron, though admittedly in this position it is less offensive, is not the best material. What is there to beat the 50 mm diameter brass tube? It seems to blend perfectly well into surroundings old or new, urban or rural, basic or 'posh'. It is essential to relate it properly to the *elbow*, as this is the only dimension strictly relevant to one's comfort. A sketch to illustrate this important point is given on p. 146.

Machinery

What can one say of the miscellaneous, extraneous, intercutaneous infestation of juke boxes, one-armed bandits, pin tables and amusement machines which now buzz, click, bleep, chatter and caterwaul in almost every bar of the land? Like vermin they multiply, and like parasites they threaten the essential bodily functions on which the health of the pub must depend.

First, they offer no welcome. At the door one is repulsed by an aggressive bombardment of sound. They abolish seclusion. How can one find sanctuary in a raucous din? The basis of friendliness is conversation, and this they destroy. Strident noise penetrates the soul's defences, provokes bitterness, and utterly disperses goodheartedness. Nor is their appearance any better then their cacophonous assault on the ears. Chromium plate, shocking pink and luminous sick-green vie with flashing lights and restless movement to numb the eye's response to its surroundings.

Worst of all, perhaps, from the brewer's point of view, is the undeniable fact that they skim the cream of the cash into others' pockets. How is it that they are willing to contemplate the steady erosion of the volume of sales for the sake of the immediate profit to be gained from incidental and irrelevant gimmickry? Brewery management seem to have overlooked the simple fact that if Jock and Bill go out in the evening with a fiver to spend, and two pounds go into the box or bandit, that is 40 per cent less into the cash register, quite apart from the pounds which would have been spent by others who recoiled from the racket and took themselves home. Enormous investment in production capacity and distribution resources becomes ever less viable when volume declines, while brewing staff and draymen alike are faced with the eventual prospect of redundancy.

What's to be done? History, as usual, provides the answer. Hitherto, whenever a trend has developed to the point where it became incompatible with the pub's definitive nature it has been firmly set aside. Market, music hall, gentlemen's club – all began in pubs and are now accommodated elsewhere. Let there be pin-table parlours, halls of amusement, discotoria by all means. Let them even be licensed. But please don't bring this nonsense into the people's pubs. What is the sense of destroying the one to gain the others? Open new establishments, certainly, to cater for all tastes, but not at the expense of a known and existing asset, our incomparable drinking places. Whoever deprives us of these will not be forgiven.

A Note about Maintenance

The more one becomes accustomed to looking closely at the minuscule details of a bar's appearance the more obvious it is that quite small flaws can add up to something abhorrent, and that most of these are due to the neglect of maintenance and cleaning. I illustrate this point by quoting below from a description, written in the early 1960's, of an imaginary but by no means untypical 19th-century inner-ring London pub:

"A first glance conveys something of the grandiose scale of the place as it once was. The patterned brown ceiling covers the whole public space including the servery, and the tall fluted columns with composite capitals tower above the U-shaped counter: but in one corner a few square feet of the original anaglypta has been damaged by a burst pipe, and replaced with pale pink plaster devoid of paint. Pallid spheres of light hang at wide intervals over our heads, and two fluorescent tubes fed by festoons of flex have been added behind the counter. The monumental cornice of the carved mahogany backfitting has been encased in reeded hardboard, and the acid-etched mirrors behind the shelves are covered with coat on coat of cream paint. Observe the display – no riotous assembly of sparkling coloured bottles and polished casks here, but a few dusty beer bottles, faded advertisement cards, and paper doyleys. The counter itself is covered with pink plastic, and its panelled mahogany front is painted two shades of grey. The walls of the public bar are still lined with matchboarding, but it has been done over some years ago with a sickly yellowish graining, and in the Saloon there is a pink and white paper of modern design, more than slightly soiled now, and peeling away around the fireplace.

"The fireplace! Here stood an overmantel of polished, carved mahogany and French embossed mirrors over a heavy marble plinth. Now it is a domestic hearth of little beige tiles, some of them cracked and kicked away; and in the fire opening no blazing coals, but an ancient advertisement for cigarettes.

"Clusters of black fluff hang stickily from the plaster cornice. There is dust on the clock. The brilliant-cut glass partitions are all gone – all except one, in which two panes have been replaced with two different patterns of lavatory glass. The curtains droop. The upholstery sags. The cast-iron tables have been banished to the yard, and new, cheap, wooden ones with yellow plastic tops stand on the torn, green, rubber-tiled floor. A heap of orange-coloured bottle cases stands in the servery, and on it hang the damp tea-towels. In the back room a flickering, nattering television set destroys the last vestige of comfort or delight which a stranger might have hoped he would find."

Nothing could be less welcoming, less convivial, less good-hearted than the kind of place thus described: and they still exist. How is it that otherwise fairly shrewd business people, the owners, allow such horrors to remain? One reason may be that they just don't look. The area or district manager is too much preoccupied with mundane matters such as stock, ullage, point-of-sale material, cellar temperature and the licensee's wife's lumbago, all of which claim his attention on a routine visit, with many more. The licensee, for his part, being there every day, simply fails to notice the gradual accretions of squalor. Another factor might be that a tenant has abandoned hope because of illness, old age, bureaucratic bumbledom or general discouragement. Managers, however, are exposed far too often to an additional and unnecessary pressure, relentlessly applied by the brewery director, in the matter of staff wages.

The rot sets in when remote accountants, noses glued to their print-outs, initiate a nation-wide cut in allocations of funds both for repairs and for furnishing replacements. Shabbiness sets in, the customers feel affronted, and the trade falls off. Area managers, looking at their books instead of their bars, decree that the wages bill must be cut in its turn. More often than not this means that time spent on cleaning is greatly reduced. The place begins to look still more unkempt, trade falls still further, and again the wages bill must be cut. A downward spiral is in progress. The remedy is only too obvious, but how often do we find it applied? A thorough wash and a 'coat of polish' is the first thing we need. Only a bar which someone cares for sufficiently to keep it gleaming can create in the customer a feeling that he, too, is well-loved. Surely this is a relatively inexpensive way of ensuring that he stays a little longer, and returns more frequently.

6 Lighting

Although there exists no generally accepted scientific language with which to describe the quality or mood of lighting, it is surely obvious that we can, by planning the intensity, colour, distribution and direction of light sources, express many different mental attitudes and conditions, including those which are relevant to social drinking – the welcome, the seclusion, the informality and even the goodheartedness. Indeed, it may be truer still to say that by ill-chosen, badly arranged lighting these feelings can be dispersed. In other words, by means of lighting it is possible largely to create or completely to destroy the atmosphere we require. Unfortunately, lighting remains the design component in which failure is most often seen.

Intensity

Possibly such failures most often result from paying too much attention to lighting engineers, who have been mainly concerned with the provision of optimum intensities of light for various practical 'tasks', rather than the use of lighting to induce human reactions. My impression is that they tend to aim at the delivery of equal and even illumination to all parts of a surface, or of a room. This may be all right for a workshop, a public library, a department store or an office, but a moment's thought will show that it is hardly an adequate guide for anyone involved in the design of a lighting scheme for, let us say, a theatre, or a dance hall, or even a shop window. When it comes to the design of a drinking environment I am convinced that it is in fact the precise opposite of what is required. I quote, in support of this contention, the American lighting designer, Leslie Larson, whose book *Lighting and its Design* was published in 1964 by the Whitney Library of Design, New York. He writes: "An environment enlivened by *variation* (my italics) is stimulating and is of constant interest, while a space too evenly lit and lacking defining shadows is simply a bore . . ." I will return to the matter of shadows a little later. Larson goes on: "Lighting which is flat as a result of too great diffusion is depressing regardless of its intensity."

"Regardless of its intensity." If this is right, and I insist that it is, it makes nonsense of the parrot-cry so often encountered. "The place is gloomy, let us have more light". In such a case, more light could very well make the effect worse than before. What is probably needed is not "more light" everywhere, but possibly pools of brightness (or even of relative darkness) here and there to create some variety. Once I was invited by a friend to his local, and as his favourite bar was uncomfortably crowded we went into the other. There we sat the whole evening in a glare of light and increasing discomfort, and it was noticeable that although there was a steady stream of trade (it was Saturday night) no-one except ourselves stayed very long. A succession of little groups came in, swallowed a quick one, and off they went. Then, at the cry of "Last orders", half the lights were switched off. Immediately, the atmosphere was transformed, and my feeling of relief that the evening was over was replaced by a reluctance to leave. Note, that this happy effect would not have occurred if all the lights had been dimmed to half power. Uniform brilliance would then have become uniform gloom. It was the variation of intensity given by turning off *some* of the lights which made the entire room more comfortable.

It is not difficult to see how this principle relates to the criteria of 'pubness' which I have described earlier. Uniform brightness makes the drinker feel exposed and vulnerable and destroys his seclusion. The strident glare of light is far from welcoming. Any shortcomings in the shape of the space are emphasised. Uniform dimness, on the other hand, can create gloom: but it is the uniformity as much as the dimness which has that effect. In either case the lack of contrast or shadows, which are needed to give visual interest and quality to the contents of the room, will result in dullness and monotony. The very word 'monotony' means, of course, 'all of one tone', and in a bar this is precisely what we must avoid. It is worth noting here that proper shadows are only provided by point sources of light. The sun, because of its distance from the earth, is virtually a point source of light, and gives crisp, sharp-edged, well-defined shadows. The diffused light of an overcast sky is, by contrast (or, rather, through lack of contrast) gloomy. In the same way, diffused artificial light is depressing: a tube light, being a linear source, gives blurred shadows, and panels of light, being plane sources, give hardly any shadows at all. In such conditions every object loses its three-dimensional quality; the room appears flat and lacking in interest. The reason for this becomes obvious when you consider that an artist, wishing to portray on a flat canvas the roundness of an apple as opposed to a plate, does so by means of shading.

Uniform and diffused lighting also tend to dispel one's goodhearted-ness, in that too much brilliance will induce a mood of defiance, and too little will result in despair. Again, what is needed is variation of intensity, so that neither extreme is inflicted. Larson, again, says that correct lighting "should range from excitement to repose. Actually a quantity of both in varying combinations should make up all seeing situations." A bit of a mouthful, certainly, but how right! How accurately this describes an atmosphere for social drinking. If either component is lacking the bar will be wrong, and I believe that an important ingredient of success in designing a pub is the achievement of the correct balance between 'repose' and 'stimulation'. This balance is not the same in the different 'levels' of bar, a subtle matter which is examined in another chapter.

Once it is accepted that our aim must be to design a lighting scheme which gives, by means of variation, a proper balance between stimulation and repose, the reason why certain kinds of installation normally fail becomes clear immediately. We can rule out, for a start, plane sources of light overhead. Illuminated ceilings are obviously a nonsense, whether they are luminous plastic panels, egg-crate arrangements, or simply light thrown upwards from a trough on to white or pale-coloured plaster. Of all methods of lighting these are the most diffused, the most lacking in shadows and in variation. Furthermore, being overhead, they make the ceiling look like a sky – the symbol of all we have come in to get away from. In fact the ceiling is the last place where light is required. Nobody counts his change there, or reads the paper. In tall rooms especially, light on the ceiling attracts attention upwards and emphasises the height. Thus, in both ways, seclusion is lost and 'atmosphere' is dispelled.

An effect almost as unfortunate can be given by the naked fluorescent tube: here I must own up to the fact that there was once a one bar lit in this way where I myself frequently drank. Its other remarkable qualities sufficed to override the sad effect of the lighting. I am content to accept this case as the exception which proves the rule: but it may be worth mentioning that this particular bar was one of great visual strength – a long, fairly low 'tunnel' with a window at each end, several assorted iron columns and a ceiling of nicotined tongued and grooved boards. It may therefore be right to suggest that the characterless and flabby lighting was overcome by the splendid toughness of the room. However, the vast majority of bars can be totally ruined by the installation of these crude, illiterate sticks of milk-coloured light, whether they are slapped straight on to the ceiling or suspended some distance below. Even the colours in the room are distorted, because this type of light is deficient in the red and yellow components of the spectrum, reducing warm browns in the direction of grey. Most of the drawbacks of plane sources also apply. In my opinion, for all these reasons, it is best to avoid altogether the use of fluorescent light, unless it is placed in inverted troughs in such a way that the light is thrown downwards and the tubes are concealed.

Colour

If we can agree that a variety of tungsten light sources is the only acceptable main illumination for a bar, we have still to consider colour, and if as I have suggested, it is a mistake to use surfaces which are cold in colour, it must follow that blue or green lighting will have an equally chilling effect; because obviously the look of a surface is a product of its hue and the context of lighting in which it is seen. Cold coloured light will cancel out the effect of materials, wallpapers or paint chosen for the contribution they can make to a warm welcome. Even a single blue or green *lamp* can throw off balance a well designed arrangement of light, and this, of course, is a matter for control by management. Similarly, it would be absurd to choose translucent shades which throw a cold blue light over everything in view. However, there is a type of green *shade* which can, in limited numbers, be used to provide an 'accent' of vivid colour, enhancing by contrast all the warmth of the surroundings, and introducing a note of controlled liveliness. This can only be done if the shades are open at the bottom, so that 90% of the light from each point is directed downwards into the room, and the shades are seen merely as patches of coloured surface, rather than as sources of coloured light.

Indeed, it is true that whatever colours are chosen the direct light of an ordinary tungsten lamp should be allowed to escape downwards. Colour, in other words, should be in the shade and not in the lamp. Direct light seems to be necessary for our appreciation of the quality of any object, and since we do not want direct light in our eyes the obvious solution is to control the direct light in a downwards direction, which is what shades are for. Many otherwise excellent bars have been to some extent spoiled by using too many coloured lamps. The effect of unrelieved pink, amber or red light everywhere, though certainly warm, is nevertheless gloomy and in some way depressing. Even where a 'smoochy' atmosphere is acceptable a certain amount of direct light is needed to enliven the scene.

Distribution

So we are faced with the job of arranging the distribution in the room of a number of point sources of light. It may at first seem quite a simple matter to dot the fittings about the plan at one for every so many square metres; but there are snags. For a start, someone else will be replacing the lamps. Too few points, and they will put in lamps of enormous wattage which assault the vision and may damage the fittings. Too many, and some of the fittings will finish up with no lamps in at all, frustrating the designed effect and giving a look of neglect, like a mouth with missing teeth. In order to avoid too even a spread of illumination it is commonsense to provide a greater concentration of light where practical purposes require it, that is, in the servery, where people want to count their change, and where the staff have to work. This ensures, too, that attention is drawn towards the bar, which is the focus of activity and the source of supply; but again, a nice balance is needed to avoid too sharp a line of separation between those serving and those served. I have seen a room where the area behind the counter, being bathed in white light, looked like a brilliant shop window in a darkened street, or like the stage of a theatre, while the public space, with warm shaded wall fittings, receded into comparative obscurity.

There are great advantages in wall fittings. If the bar is a suitable shape it may be possible to avoid the use of overhead light altogether, except, of course, in large squarish rooms where the middle of the floor could be totally unlit. The wall brackets should be placed as low as practicable: over

68

seating, fixed tables or shelves they can be well below eye level, which is useful because it is not enough to ensure a proper distribution of sources in the horizontal plane: they must also be arranged at different levels above the floor. I have already pointed out the reasons for avoiding too much light on the ceiling, and the reason for not placing lights too high is that they will attract attention upwards, which has an ill effect on the apparent proportion of the room; but if every fitting is suspended at precisely the same height the appearance will lack variety and interest. So it is always a good idea to have fittings of different types – pendants, wall brackets, downlighters, standard lamps and so on, at different levels in the vertical plane.

Direction

As already mentioned, the main objection to light from both plane and linear sources is precisely that it is indiscriminate in direction. There is nowhere in the room from which the source cannot be seen. Its radiation is uncontrolled, and spreads as evenly on every surface as butter on bread. Surely this is a naive, even an ignorant way of using artificial light. Hardly better in this respect than panels and tubes are plain white spheres or 'footballs'. Beloved of early Modern Movement perspectivists, these unimaginative globes have been thoughtlessly inflicted upon us ever since by many designers. They are only one degree less crude than a bare lamp: and I look forward to the day when lamps clearly visible from any normal viewpoint will be regarded as no less obscene than the public display of one's private organs.

Opal globes conceal the lamp, but give a flat and dismal appearance. Clear glass and crystal shades are really neither better nor worse. Their one tiny advantage is that they can give a bit of sparkle, and if a clear lamp is used its outline is camouflaged so that all one sees is a glitter of light; but if too large a lamp is used this becomes dazzle, while if it is replaced by a pearl one all is revealed, as though by a see-through shift (– and much less attractively!). To my mind, careful thought is needed before this type of fitting is decided upon, simply because it can be so badly misused by insensitive staff. For the same reason, dimmers are dangerous. It may be tempting to think it a good idea to make the level of light adjustable, so that the licensee may vary it to suit the mood of the gathering, or of the time of day, but in practice what seems to happen is that it is turned up to maximum brightness for the cleaners in the morning, and remains a glaring assault on the eyes of the customers all day long.

The subject of dazzle is one which needs further investigation. I have seen bars (or at any rate one) where the improbable feat was achieved of combining dazzle with an overall illumination so inadequate as to be funereal. Clear bare lamps of very low wattage could be seen through the front glass of antique coach lamps fixed to the wall exactly at eye level. No other light was provided except a little behind the counter. Against the darkness of the background the tiny lamps appeared intolerably bright, and I assume that this was because the pupil had adjusted to the relative

69

Britannia tables in the Olde Bull & Bush, Hampstead, painted gilt and equipped with gallery rails. In fact these rails can be a bit of a nuisance to drinkers, but this is a small price to pay for their delightful appearance.

Tetley's Vittle Inns provide a drinking environment which is both traditional and (apart from a few loose ornaments) belongs quite distinctly to the last quarter of the twentieth century.

This little Snob Screen at Hollands, London, E.1. is a charming bit of visual incident: not by any means a serious barrier between 'them' and 'us'.

To meet local demand a strong nicotine brown was applied to this ceiling in the 1950's; now it has been repainted a pale biscuit colour, an unnecessary carpet has been fitted, and the counter panels have been overlaid with red velvet.

Two 'English' pubs in Rotterdam (opposite and right).

Arches (below) link the original Victorian bar with a sympathetic modern extension; they are echoed by mirrored arches on the far wall, and so an extremely satisfying labyrinthine effect is created.

An interior by
Mayell Hart &
Partners at the
Apollo, Marylebone.

(Right) An old
'tram-seat' renovated
and installed in an
English pub in
Rotterdam (together
with a glazed screen,
a pub table and two
carved stools).

Materials, colours
and detail add up to
a satisfying, mellow
and almost timeless
ambience which (even
without the optic and
the one-armed bandit)
could only be 'Pub'.

A quite agreeable Brewers' Tudor treatment somewhat marred by the intrusion of a factory type clock—with its tatty bit of wiring.

The famous collection of customers' ties at the Bear, Oxford. No blank wall spaces here! And what could be more satisfying than the diagonally boarded counter front, the pewter top and the splendid row of china beer-pump handles with their moulded brass mounts?

Design flair. The Chestnut Tree, Leytonstone, an alteration for Ind Coope Ltd, by Roderick Gradidge. Surprise and delight are carefully blended to make an unusually exciting pub interior.

The false ceiling extending from left to right not only divides the room into three parts (near, higher: middle, lower: and far, higher) but also provides a visual link between the servery and the public space.

Victorian engineering is preferable to modern marketing-type dispense equipment.

Although the decorative wall mirrors could perhaps be criticised as lacking toughness, the general effect of this modern Public Bar at Redditch provides a hard, smooth, brown environment, and is a worthy successor to generations of taprooms, vaults and 'four-ale-bars'.

Fine Edwardian buttoned seating restored with Draylon, in a house which had been damaged by fire. To my mind this room is not improved by the overhead skylight, and it could certainly do with some suitable bric-a-brac on the green area of wall.

Lino can hardly be bettered for a public bar floor, but it must be kept as well polished as this one. (The boarded back seats are quite in keeping, but some of the loose furniture could be improved upon).

The geometric curve of the counter top not only provides elbow-leaning space for numerous customers without giving the staff too far to walk while serving, but also permits them to face inwards towards each other and converse in friendly fashion without the need to raise their voices.

Real pub components: the brush-grained panelled counter front, and its moulded hardwood top; the corniced rear display fitting; the little glazed screens on the top of the counter; and the slender cast-iron column. Just outside the picture is a tongued, grooved and bead-moulded dado.

An honest Public Bar in Derby, which is unassuming and all the more satisfying for that.

Superb decorative mirrors were salvaged from the French Horn and Half Moon in Wandsworth, when it was demolished, and installed in this North London pub.

This Tap Room is certainly a 'symphony in brown', and how right.

7 Distinctions Between Bars

All that I have tried to do, up to this point, is to show that it is possible to recognise and retain in good pubs, of any type or period including the present, those essential characteristics which have run through all the growth and change, and which distinguish pubs from other places. The logical extension of this process is to consider the various rooms in the pub and see what it is that distinguishes them from each other.

It is clear from the historical background expounded by Maurice Gorham and H. McG. Dunnett in *Inside The Pub* that the basic pub room, variously referred to as Public Bar, Tap Room, and in the north Vaults or Vault, is directly descended from the kitchen of the inn, and from the tap room of the tavern where the casks were stored. These rooms were the resorts of the least exalted rank of patrons, labourers, packhorse drivers, waggoners and others with no social pretensions. Gentry were accommodated in the Coffee Room of the inn, and in the parlour or inner private room of the tavern. From these more exclusive places the Saloon Bar and northern Smoke Room evolved. It is convenient to refer to these two types, with their roots in the past, as 'Pub Rooms Proper', while more recently accepted innovations such as Lounges (which began in hotels), the 20's and 30's Cocktail Bars, American Bars and suchlike, may be referred to for lack of a better term as 'Smart Rooms'. Of course it is true that nowadays a good many rooms in two-bar pubs are known as 'Lounges', mainly because the owners feel that this can justify a higher price range. However, when considering a bar's appeal in terms of its visual qualities, I suggest that it is better to keep the older meaning of the word for the sake of the distinction, and throughout I shall use the word 'Lounge' in the sense which, when it was first applied to pub rooms and for decades afterwards, very nearly always meant the third or fourth level of trading room. Only the existence of a Private Bar or Snug of some sort would make it the fourth, because these two departments were normally slotted in between the Public and the Saloon, the former often in a geographical as well as a social sense. Large Victorian pubs, despite their multiplicity of *bars*, I suppose to have had only three *levels*, corresponding to Public, Private and Saloon. In Mark Girouard's scholarly book, *Victorian Pubs*, there is no reference to Lounges, from which I think it may be assumed that even if the social divisions were as numerous as the bars, not even the highest achieved the status of Lounge. Possibly this was one reason for the later phenomenon of pubs which were 'hotels' only in name – an attempt to overcome the lack of esteem with which the middle classes regarded the pub, and to extend the social range of its clientele. It is, in a way, a pity that this praiseworthy object should have had so confusing an effect on nomenclature.

Now, few would deny that in the latter half of the 20th century all this talk of class is anachronistic. Why, you may say, bother to make distinctions now that the class stratification is being abandoned? Why speak of Public, Private, Saloon and Lounge when the one-bar pub is now for many reasons often preferred? My answer is that, just as the customer requires a pub to be recognisable as such, so he is accustomed to find, in the bar he frequents, an atmosphere which is in certain essentials familiar. If it lacks the peculiar flavour *of its type*, the bar will fail to satisfy, and probably without quite knowing why, the customer will leave and seek in some other place the fulfilment of his rather subtle subconscious requirements.

Although social conditions change, characteristics which originated deep in the past, and which have endured for so long, become ingrained in the consciousness – long after their original meaning has been forgotten or superseded, their effects, because they have become familiar and are so much part of our lives, are accepted as right and proper. Any departure from them which is made too abruptly will be resented. Change we must have, but we must be careful that it is neither too violent nor too sudden, lest we antagonise the people in a way they could not themselves clearly define.

We should remember, too, that we are not at the end of a tradition, but at an intermediate point from which we can look forward as well as back. By making our own contribution we can take the process one stage farther. If we try to halt it and start again we are likely to fail. It is no more possible to make a clean sweep of familiar environments than it would be to abolish the language and invent a new one tomorrow, from scratch: communication would instantly cease, and in the same way interiors (for almost any purpose) which completely lack the element of reminiscence will not be recognised for what they are attempting to be. This is no less true of the 'levels' of bar than of the whole pub itself.

So, although the customer's choice of room depends less and less on class with the passage of time, he will still choose different bars according to his mood, and because moods vary we shall still require a possible choice between two or three different styles of drinking room. In the 1970's many pubs were built and rebuilt in such a way that certain people at certain times and in certain moods (or dressed in certain ways, because dress and mood interact) could find no bar in which they felt at home. They felt, in other words, out of place: and this is a thing we can only avoid by retaining, not perhaps in every pub but surely in most, at least two bars, *or sections of a bar*, offering different styles of environment which are, in their essentials, familiar to those who want them.

It is, of course, in the Pub Rooms Proper rather than the Smart Rooms that we can see reflected the growth and change which have taken place so far. These are the rooms which have been going longest and from which we have most to learn. Many have been destroyed by injudicious modernisation, and where relatively untouched examples exist they should therefore be cherished. Fortunately there are signs that more brewers and designers are coming to realise that it is absurd to replace sound old well-built and well-designed components (such as natural timber, brush-grained matchboarding, polished brass and decorated or mirrored glass) with less durable finishes lacking both character and robustness. Let us hope that they can also educate the brash young tenant-licensee and his wife whose hasty and ill-considered depredations can still be a menace.

However, it is not by any means only the older interiors which have the authentic flavour. In the third quarter of the century quite a number of bars were created where the real pub look was achieved by means of well-chosen materials and an absence of anything obviously contrived or false. These too deserve protection from vandals. Their unobtrusive appeal comes from an easy relationship of the parts to each other and to the whole; and it is as important to the till as it is to the eye.

Public Bars

For a fuller understanding of the architectural detail associated with the basic pub room I can do no better than refer professional readers to the words and illustrations in Gorham and Dunnett's book *Inside the Pub*. My purpose here is just to draw attention to the general effect of this type, and the demand for it which comes from social drinkers in a 'Public Bar' mood. At one time there was in the trade an obsession with the idea that it was desirable to 'upgrade' such bars by softening their character with curtains, carpets, and light, bright colours to appeal to an imaginary suburban taste, and this process was invariably followed by an increase in price. To my mind, this attitude to prices is irrelevant and illusory. With the possible exception of some whose misfortune it is to live in industrially depressed areas, people do not make the price of drinks a major factor in choosing their bar. They know what they like, and an extra penny a half-pint is not going to deter them. What does put them off is to find a prim and genteel withdrawing-room in place of their familiar and unassuming surrounding.

Nor can the basic bar ever be regarded as a Smoke Room or Saloon done on the cheap. It may well, in fact, be *more* expensive to build, but it does not ape the characteristics of the bar next door. It is its own uncompromising self, with a rather sophisticated hardness and smoothness appropriate to its kitchen tradition. It has an honest-to-goodness, down-to-earth character, a restrained masculinity and a controlled strength. Its detail has a clarity and honesty which may quite well be lacking in other rooms. There is nothing archaic about it. The furnishings and finishes will be of a high standard and

73

can be thoroughly up-to-date, but if they have not the distinctive flavour that belongs to the bar, the result will fail to appeal to the appropriate mood. That this mood is commoner and more widespread than anyone (in the brewery office) thinks, is testified by many public bars I have known, in widely differing areas, where the demand for such a bar has been met, and where favourable customer reaction has greatly increased trade.

As Gorham and Dunnett have pointed out, even the urban Public Bar retains some hint of its origin, something of the feel of an old country kitchen. This is mainly in the materials and colours, as they say, but it is also true that its spatial qualities seem to show less of the intricate subdivision proper to other bars. Ray Carter noticed that Public Bar customers tend to form a single group, and have a habit of calling out to each other in matey fashion from one side of the bar to another. This is surely appropriate kitchen behaviour, and it implies that in the design of this bar it is less important to provide semi-secluded cubicles for self-contained groups. However, seclusion from the outside world is still needed, and it is just as necessary here to avoid large areas of vacant floor space – a fault almost universal in pubs of the 30's.

It is undoubtedly the enclosing surfaces which provide the chief distinguishing characteristic of the basic pub room. Too much softness of appearance is obviously out of place here; but although the effect is certainly hard it is a smooth, rounded hardness, warm, sympathetic, tough rather than rough. Nothing is crude, harsh or splintered. In the chapter on 'surfaces' I have already extolled the merits of tongued, grooved and bead-moulded matchboarding, and this material, correctly detailed and coloured, offers the most infallible means of achieving the recognisable Public Bar look. Quite a few such bars were designed as recently as the 1960's and 1970's, notably by Basil Sugden and Tony Sobierajski. It is hard to imagine an authentic Public without at least one matchboarded element, whether it is the ceiling, dado, counter front or seat backs. Boards need not be all of the same width, though self-consciously 'random' effects are better avoided. It is also helpful to vary the direction of the boards, and horizontal fixing is ideal for seat backs especially, since only in this way can the back be shaped to give the greater comfort of a bulge for lumbar support. Even diagonal boarding is appropriate in particular contexts, such as counter front panels, and this I think is true despite its somewhat 'chapel' associations!

Traditionally, the colours which *predominate* in this type of bar constitute what Lewis Mumford referred to as a "symphony in brown". I understand that he applied this phrase to the whole pub, but although I would myself be very happy in a totally brown pub this is surely too restrictive for universal application. Nevertherless, in the basic bar this relative restriction is not only useful but essential. The word I have stressed is 'predominate'. Limited amounts of other colours can of course be used without detriment, as long as they are not shades incompatible with the pub scene as a whole. I remember getting rather cross with a colleague of mine who ordered a vivid red curtain to form a sort of lobby at the street door of a

Public Bar, but it turned out that he was right, because the quantity of red was not excessive compared with the extent of the rest of the room, which was coloured in different shades and tones of brown, except for a single central column improbably painted blue; and this, too, succeeded as a touch of contrast to accentuate the quality and colour of the natural timber. It is remarkable how many people, when this idea of a virtually monochrome bar is put to them, recoil from it in fright. They fear that the result will be monotonous. How can it possibly be '*monotonous*', when by definition one is choosing a multitude of *tones*? It is not the tones but the shade, or 'chrome', which is 'mono'! Nor is there, in fact, any sameness about brown. Since it is not in the spectrum, and therefore not a 'real' colour, but a combination of colours, it has a greater variety than any of them. Browns can range not only from pale straw to bog oak, from light ale to stout, but also from reddish-brown through yellowish-brown to greenish-brown, which is known as khaki. Even a blueish brown is conceivable, though not necessarily to be recommended. When one considers also the wide choice available of material, texture and degree of lustre it is clear that what might at first appear to threaten monotony in fact does nothing of the sort. The very word 'symphony' in Mumford's phrase suggests otherwise.

Another characteristic of the basic bar is that surfaces, colours and materials are generally paler than their counterparts in the Saloon. This may possibly be due to more expensive, darker and mellower timber having been used in the more expensive bar, and probably the monochrome itself arose from the fact that any surface in a kitchen or bar, whatever its original colour, will tend to take on a smoke or nicotine shade if left untouched for a while. It may be that in earlier days the kitchen and tap were decorated less frequently than the parlour. However, the reasons are less important than that we should be able to find and to recognise, whether or not with awareness, the appropriate style or appearance which has become attached to a particular drinking mood. This is what gives the visual distinctions their relevance.

Similarly, the contents of the basic bar are by no means identical with those in other parts of the pub. Softness and luxury do not fit the scene. Frilliness and fussiness cannot be tolerated. Curtains, for instance, may very well not be needed at all, but if for any reason they must be provided let them be relatively simple and plain, eschewing the floral patterns, the scalloped edges and the ruched whatsisnames. Carpet is normally out of the question;* but again, in a particular case it may just conceivably be accepted, provided that it covers only a minor area of the floor, and that it is neither fancy nor lush. For floor covering surely a choice can be made from among the harder materials – stone flags, quarry tiles, boards or linoleum, depending on the style and situation of the house. Nor do we need a vast amount of stuff hung on the wall. Here the filling of vacant spaces must be

* There may still be localities with a history of underprivilege where, owing to the swing of the pendulum, carpet is at present demanded in every bar. In the opposite sort of district, e.g. Belgravia, it will hardly be tolerated even in the lounge.

done with great subtlety. A large mirror is probably splendid if the frame is not too ornate. Notice boards also perform this additional useful function. Posters are acceptable if not allowed to get too scrofulous. For the rest, restraint is needed. In any case a matchboarded wall, because of its own visual texture and patina, is less offensive than paint or paper even if nothing is put on it at all.

It is certainly the lighting of the Public Bar which gives the greatest difficulty. Rather a lot of careful thought is needed in order to steer a middle course between too much elaboration and, on the other hand, anything too obviously cheap and nasty. Straightforward, simple fittings of good quality are probably best, if they can be found. There is a demand in this bar for a somewhat higher general level of illumination than in the others, partly because the customers do like to see each other's faces (not necessarily true of the Saloon) and also because one must be able to play dominoes as well as darts, and to read the evening paper. However, it is still essential to ensure a variation of intensity from one part of the bar to another. One way to think of the problem is to say that, starting from the same median level, the Public will need some areas of brighter light, and the Saloon some with areas where it is more subdued.

To conclude these remarks on the basic pub room, the following little story seems to me to have relevance. In the Double Diamond in Rotterdam, where the brief was to convert a restaurant into a typical English pub, a tiny section of the single compartmented ground-floor bar was treated as a Public, with boarded floor, matchboarded walls and counter front, and pewter counter top. Everything was in tones of brown, and the furniture was real pub stuff, kitchen-type tables with turned legs and a renovated old tram seat. One day four or five Dutch painters in white overalls entered the main door in the carpeted Saloon Bar part, looked hesitantly to right and left, and finally moved decisively through the Private, with its lino floor, and took up their position in the little Public, confident that they had found the part of the pub where they did not feel out of place; this despite the fact that they were Dutch and had never heard of a Public Bar. Indeed, the price level was the same throughout the pub.

Smoke Rooms/Saloon Bars

In this sub-section I am including any so-called Lounge in a pub where the only bar is a Public Bar or Tap Room. To my mind, the second room in any pub automatically falls into this category, unless a conscious decision has been made to have no Public at all, in which case the two rooms will be Saloon and Lounge, or even Lounge A and Lounge B: but I do not believe that there are many situations where such a decision would be justified. Surely it is foolhardy to throw aside the commercial benefits to be gained from the established attitudes of customers. In Birmingham as early as the 1960's there was a trend to do away entirely with the 'middle' bar, and in a two-room pub there would be one which was not only called but looked like a lounge, and another labelled simply 'Bar'. This one became something of a hybrid, lacking the physical comfort of the Lounge, the mellowness of the Smoke Room and the traditional colouring of the Public Bar. It is questionable whether anybody really liked it. No doubt, *faute de mieux*, it was used, because most surviving Public Bars in Birmingham at that time were pretty dreadful. Certainly the loss of the intermediate 'level' was a serious one, especially in commercial districts such as shopping streets, where the suburban gentility of the lounges never seemed a suitable setting for the business people's midday or early evening couple of jars. I did find one middle bar which, because of its interior treatment, I unhesitatingly placed in the Smoke Room bracket. It was called the Gun Room, and in the same pub there was also a good hard Public with a brown quarry tiled floor, which was fairly well used, and a lush lounge which was not, at any rate in the lunch-time session. This was an area with plenty of shops, offices and banks, and the Gun Room exactly suited the type of trade thus generated. Unfortunately nobody at the time took much notice of the object lesson, which could have been applied with benefit to other places in Birmingham.

One may, I think, for practical purposes, ignore any distinction between the Smoke Room and the Saloon Bar. These are mainly regional terms, and there need be little if any difference of style, except to cater for relatively superficial regional tastes. It is true that many northern Smoke Rooms had no counter, so that customers had to serve themselves from a bar or hatch in a passage, and there was no perpendicular drinking within the room: but this is an inconvenient and unsociable arrangement which need not be mourned, and for purposes of design it seems reasonable to regard the two types as one. Both share a descent from the licensee's private parlour, and it is natural that the degree of seclusion proper to such a room should be perpetuated. Since the parlour was small and many Saloon Bars are pretty extensive, this is normally achieved by means of subdivisions, alcoves, cubicles – whatever you like to call the semi-secluded areas to which I have already referred in the chapter on spatial qualities. A Snug, which is by definition the ultimate in seclusion, bears still more resemblance to the old parlour itself. Some were reserved for regulars of long standing, nominated by the guv'nor for this privilege, which the rest of us must accept on the basis of tradition, but for my own part I feel it is too exclusive and unsociable, smacking of clubs rather than pubs. Spatially, the snug must of necessity be very small indeed, preferably 'behind the pumps', that is, reached only through the servery by invitation, and probably having no external window. The surfaces, contents and artificial lighting will share the characteristics of Saloon Bars, but without gimmickry.

Saloon Bars and Smoke Rooms, as might be expected, offer a shade more physical comfort than the Public as well as greater subdivision and complexity: but their main distinction is a visual richness and elaboration of surfaces and furnishings. Rosewood, mahogany or dark oak predominate. Mellower colours, deeper browns, warm reds, gleaming black, even dark bottle green – these combine with a continuity of architectural incident and a multitude of polished surfaces to provide a nice balance of reposefulness and stimulation. In the ideal Saloon Bar there would be so little wall surface actually showing that the choice of wallpaper would hardly matter: but many are too large, and especially too tall, for such quantities of embellishment, and here is a good opportunity for the use of gorgeous pattern in glowing colour. Curtains and carpet blend in to the scene, and here more than anywhere framed mirrors and mirrored areas of wall can be successful in creating the sense of mystery and involvement. This is where, if you insist, gimmick and wit may more safely be indulged than in the Public, and here the licensee's collections of whatever-it-is may be displayed. Oddments of old furniture fit in particularly well, not dotted about accidentally, but placed to show the owner's pride in a valued possession, avoiding too the standardised look which comes from too many identical stools, tables or chairs. Here will stand the grandfather clock – if you can afford the floor space – and Madam may be allowed to arrange a few flowers, provided only that their scent is not so strong as to affect the taste of the beer!

Above all, it is the lighting which can contribute to the special quality of the middle bar. Here is the greatest need for visual richness, elaboration and contrast. This is where one looks for a little sparkle, gleam and glow, and where the most generous blend of different types, colours and intensities of light can be used to give a soothing atmosphere which is not dull – a sense of stimulation which is at the same time neither brash nor crude. Direct light thrown downwards from shaded fittings into the room is then broken up and scattered by polished or lustrous surfaces reflecting it in all directions. The light is seen as points or pools of warm illumination against a somewhat darker, more subdued and intriguing background.

It is, of course, no accident that this description fits fairly exactly the common type of genuine or subtly contrived olde-worlde interior. This is a treatment which never seems to fail: the low ceiling with dark beams and joists, the burnished copper and gleaming brasswork, the plastered strip of wall above the dado covered with bits of harness, framed mirrors, weapons and what you will to such an extent that the semi-matt white painted background can hardly be seen. But note, please, that this 'formula', as I like to call it, is only one way of achieving a comparable appearance. The essential visual components need not be tied exclusively to any 'period' style. They can be designed and chosen with total indifference to teashop Tudor or brewers' Victoriana, and I claim that if the suggestions I have made are sensitively interpreted and the space, surfaces, contents and lighting are well organized, the result will be a splendid Saloon Bar.

Lounges

The introduction of lounges into pubs began as part of a laudable effort to improve the unfortunate image which the days of gin and the 1830 Beer Act had successively brought about. It was an early skirmish in the battle for respectability, which was, at the time, a worthy enough cause: but the pub is now fully accepted – victory has been gained, and it is a pity that the obsolete weapon which helped our grandfathers to win the battle still hangs round our necks and inhibits our movement. The word is an unfortunate one in the context of pubs, because it can suggest a middle-sized room in a neat detached house in the riding school belt. It conjures up a vision of gentility, discreet carpets, Regency striped wallpapers, chintz curtains, all the rigmarole of the Residents' TV lounge in a second-rate seaside temperance hotel. The drinking of a pint of beer surely demands very different surroundings from those in which one would be happy sipping tea out of delicately poised little porcelain cups.

However, it is unlikely that considerations such as these will succeed in banishing the word 'lounge' from the pub. One reason for its continued use is easy to spot. In the 1950's the word was normally applied to the third room in a pub, which was the only one to be carpeted. Always with an eye to commercial advantage, the brewers began to put up the prices in the middle bar, and in order to justify this they laid a carpet. Consequently in the eyes of brewery accountants the Saloon Bar or Smoke Room became a Lounge. This need not have mattered if only the Saloon or Smoke had continued to look and feel like one, but possibly for the reasons I have suggested this was hardly ever so, and in any case confusion was caused.

Assuming, then, that we are stuck with 'Lounges' in pubs, let us try to limit the confusion as far as possible by examining their commercial function. A lounge is historically an effort to bring into the pub a class or section of people who would not otherwise have been customers. They were accustomed to lounges in hotels and ships, but they were not at the time real pub people at all. By definition, therefore, Lounge customers are relatively unaffected by established attitudes to pub rooms. Continuity may thus be a less important factor. But surely they will not remain long to enjoy the place unless they find there the other requirements – they too will seek seclusion, welcome, friendliness and goodheartedness; or, if they do not, they must be very queer fish indeed, and it is doubtful if any licensee with his own interests at heart would wish to have them as customers.

Can we not follow on from this idea and, holding firmly to four of the five 'principles', say that the Lounge is the place for innovation? Innovation, of course, we must have. The tradition of the pub is, as I have said, one of continual change, and when change comes to a halt we shall lose the tradition: but in Pub Rooms Proper we have an asset so valuable that it must be handled delicately. At every turn the trade is faced with bright ideas, inspirations and suggestions for development from authorities, pressure groups and minorities of all kinds. This is as it should be, because however little some of the reformers may know about the pub at least they acknowledge its importance: but we do need a testing ground so that if any experiment should prove in practice to be detrimental, the ill effect may be limited in extent, and nothing of lasting value need be destroyed. What better arena could be used for this sifting process than the Lounge, by whatever name we may in the future wish to call it.

One-Bar Pubs

There are some small pubs with less than 40 m² total drinking area which are divided into two tiny bars, or even into three diminutive compartments: but for all practical purposes no bar in a normal pub is likely to be much less than 40 m², and so it is a fact that most very small pubs do in fact have only one bar. However, these are not the bars to which I am referring here. What I intend to examine is the tendency which existed in the 1960's and 70's, to amalgamate the rooms in very much larger pubs in order to create a single undifferentiated drinking room.

Up to 1964 there was a regulation which laid down that a pub possessing only one bar could be granted only a Beer and Wine Licence, permission to sell spirits as well (Full On Licences) being confined to premises which had at least two. When this restriction was removed the owners started everywhere to 'knock two bars into one', enabling them to charge one price throughout. The statutory obligation to charge low prices in Public Bars was not at that time repealed, but it was held not to apply where no Public Bar existed, and so it happened that Public Bars began to disappear, except in places where the Licensing Bench, on its own authority, insisted upon their retention. When at last the law about Public Bar prices was, in its turn, dispensed with, its effect was for a while extended in practice by a F.B.I. agreement not to raise prices by more than 5%, but this encouraged the creation of one-bar pubs, by which the agreement could be circumvented. The owner could say that he had not in fact raised his prices at all – he had merely abolished the bar in which the lower prices used to be charged, and extended the original Saloon Bar or Lounge price into a larger area. To prove it, the newly 'elevated' section of the pub was brought into line with the Saloon Bar style of furnishing and decoration, and in this way many excellent Public-Bar-style drinking places were lost.

Unfortunately, when the agreement not to raise prices expired, few if any of those concerned appeared to realise that there was no longer any reason for altering in any way the different moods for which the various sections of the pub had been designed, just because the price was to be raised.* It is my contention that few customers would complain of a single price throughout a multi-mood single bar pub, where the sections are differentiated by varying styles of furnishing, colour and lighting, to cater for different people, or for the same people on different occasions. Otherwise it is by no means impossible that the available Lounge trade will spread itself thinly in the whole of the undifferentiated pub, while potential customers in a basic bar mood take themselves elsewhere. They may even make for a club, where although their mood is not catered for at least they

---

* A further complication was later introduced by officials concerned with the control of prices and incomes, who might require evidence that capital had been spent to 'improve' a bar before authorising an increase of price—just another factor threatening the survival of a basic drinking atmosphere.

80

will not be charged extra for putting up with the carpet, and the drapes, and the upholstery.

But the application of a single price is not the only advantage to be gained by the owners of a one-bar pub. Provided it is sensitively carried out, the part-removal of screens between bars, and the formation of arches or openings in walls, can create a space which is at the same time more horizontal and more complex, closer to the ideal of a labyrinthine effect, where the customer can stroll about, without having to open or close *doors*, and choose the part which suits his mood of the moment. In this way the 'feel' of the whole place can be improved without ill effect on any part of it, convenience and flexibility of supervision and service can be improved, and customers may well be gained rather than lost. Having said this, it must once again be emphasised that a bar with a personality of its own must be delicately handled, which means that we must identify and retain in the new layout every component and relationship judged to be essential to its individual character.

8 Peripheral Cases

Clubs

It is a mystery to me why brewers continue to compete with each other to 'buy' the club trade, at enormous cost in discounts, loans and technical service, dreadfully reducing their profit margin, and allowing the clubs in their turn to compete, on thoroughly unfair terms, with the brewers' own pubs. If clubs were not subsidised in this way it would give a great boost to the Pub, which I hold to be a more valuable social asset, and a healthier one, than most clubs. This is partly because a pub is open to strangers. The general public (i.e., non-members) are legally admitted to clubs only by invitation, which means that the community at large receives no service. It also means that the man at the club bar is denied any opportunity of chance encounter with a large section of the population, any one of whom might walk into a pub.

It is naturally true that in many clubs social drinking is ancillary to the *raison d'etre* of the place, which could be squash, or gambling, or indeed anything from poodle-fancying to politics. Such establishments are certainly and quite properly legitimate, nor could one suggest that their members should not be permitted to take a drink on their premises while they relax: but the difference of emphasis clearly distinguishes them from pubs.

A more important disadvantage of clubs must be recognised, in that they are much less effectively governed by the licensing law. In proprietary clubs especially there may be attempts to dodge the system, and I believe that unless the pubs receive better support from their owners the whole drinking scene may be upset in a manner which would serve neither the public interest nor that of the Trade.

Wine Bars

While pubs have been developing more and more in the direction of lush furnishings, domestic drapes, deep carpet and soft cushions, wine bars have gone the opposite way, to the point where they now look more like pubs

82

than we often seem to achieve in the real thing. Some even have real sawdust, which has come full circle and is now almost a gimmick. Certainly it no longer suggests a 'down-market' scene. The colours in the best new wine bars are brown and cream, the seats and furniture of timber, the floor of boards or polished concrete, or covered with lino. There is an informality of style in which many find it easier to relax over their drinks than in any prissy suburban-type pub lounge. How fortunate it is that this pub quality should be preserved, no matter by whom, at a time when it has been so largely thrown away by brewers and other operators chasing extra pennies on the pint, which they mistakenly think can only be charged in sumptuous surroundings. Yet it cannot be pretended that wine bar prices are low. It is my belief that a good proportion of the wine bar trade consists of people who would marginally prefer to drink beer or spirits, but cannot find in a convenient pub the sort of atmosphere they prefer. It is sad, therefore, that wine bars, for reasons best known to themselves, nearly always refuse to serve beer. Most pubs now sell two or three different wines by the glass, and if only wine bars would offer a similarly restricted range of beers it would be a great convenience to those drinkers, normally responsible types, who would enjoy a change of scene in the course of an evening, but not if that would necessarily involve a change from grain to grape drinks, or vice versa.

And, come to think of it, why do so many wine bars seem to have the knack of serving an imaginative variety of food, without any perceptibly adverse effect on the drinking atmosphere?

Hotel Bars
Pubs which, like the White Lion Bars at the Hotel Leofric, Coventry, are built into hotels and connected only behind the scenes to the circulation of the main building, are hard to distinguish from the real thing; but in other hotels there are bars of various sorts which can be reached by the public through the hotel foyer. These I class as peripheral cases, being more noticeably ancillary to the main business of the hotel, the provision of sleeping, eating and conference accommodation. Historically, inns also accommodate guests, but in a good one nowadays one would expect a more even balance, the bars receiving emphasis at least equal to the bed and breakfast.

Although many hotel bars are well-designed drinking places* one is usually aware that they are not quite pubs. Even if the management goes out of its way to invite non-residents to use the bars there are sections of the public who will not respond, and there remains a vague feeling of exclusiveness. This may seem still worse in the winter, when only the outsiders, non-guests, are lumbered with hats and coats. There is also a tendency in hotels to dress the bar staff too smartly, in a company livery, and occasionally one may see an under-manager, in black coat and striped trousers,

---

* Especially those by the late Ken Horry, his successors and staff.

doing a stint behind the counter.* Add to this the sound of foreign waiters and kitchen staff arguing off-stage, and the effect is totally non-pub. The Royal Hotel at Cardiff once offered good examples of four different styles of hotel bar. The Cocktail Bar was entered from the monumental entrance hall, and was designed by Lupton and Morton with all the elegance and sophistication associated with this type at its best. The Dive Bar was thoroughly secluded (if not claustrophobic) in the bowels of the building. The treatment was faintly bogus olde-worlde, and it was used to some extent by the younger drinking men of the city.† Robert's Bar, named after its popular barman, was entered both from foyer and street, and offered a modern-type Saloon Bar facility to a mixed bag of customers. Best of all, in my view (though I admit bias) was the splendid Royal Bar where Gordon Godfrey and I did some furnishing in the 1950's. It remained at that time an unmistakeable Public Bar of quite exceptional grandeur, entered from the street only, and equipped with a curvilinear counter some 20 m long – an indispensable appendage on the day of a Rugby match at Arms Park.

* This was the habitual attire of a manager once appointed to a new pub in a foundry district of Sheffield. His appearance was sadly at odds with that of his clientele; nor did he understand the cellar cooling plant. The tenant who used to keep the previous pub on the same site wore a shirt with no collar, let alone tie, and always served the beer in perfect condition.

† It was here that I first became aware of the South Welshman's peculiar dedication to beer, as a pastime. Three male customers ordered three consecutive rounds of pints. When the first man ordered his second (the fourth) round I realised that these three were stuck for the rest of the evening. In London, where they treat their drinking as a link activity, incidental to some other occupation, that would have been the moment for moving on, the signal for dispersal to homes, restaurants or theatres. Immediately I felt more at home in Cardiff! It is not so much that the South Wales drink to excess – rather it is a humorously sly but wholehearted approach to the enjoyment of drinking that endears them to me. Of all my good drinking friends over the years, in other places, I think a majority must have been from that area.

9 Exteriors

Only the dourest non-traveller among pub-users will be spared the experience of finding himself in a district strange to him, looking for a port of call. This is the situation which gives rise to what is called the Casual Trade: but the degree of casualness with which a potential customer will approach his choice of pub will vary with circumstances. It depends upon whether he is driving, cycling, or on foot, and on the proximity of 'closing time'. Given a sufficiently early hour, and a reasonable number of pubs from which to choose within a feasible radius, it will then become purely a matter of personal preference. Does he like his pubs large, middling, or small; quiet or noisy; modest or 'posh'? No doubt his mind will be scanning and sifting the outward indications. The Brewers are not unaware of this fact, and indeed they go to some trouble to attract the casual drinker's attention. Until about 1977 they seemed to concentrate on presenting the organisation rather than the pub. But then it was noticed that there are more people who develop a strong dislike of one brew than who go about looking for a particular brewer's houses. 'They will accept anyone's beer except Bloggs'. When a fictional brewery called Grotny's was much castigated by a consumer organisation the firm whom this uncomfortable cap most closely fitted went to great lengths to vary the look of their houses to make them unrecognisable. Again, others, threatened in any area by a reaction against their near-monopoly, would resurrect the old name and style of a local brewery long ago absorbed into their group. Not for the first time, accepted theories of salesmanship were overturned and contradicted by pub customers' perverse behaviour!

But, when all is said and done, it is to everyone's advantage that the building should, first of all, be identifiable as a pub. In his book *Buildings and Prospects* published in 1948, John Piper offered a number of thoughts on this intriguing subject which I recommend for careful study by all concerned. Here is a sample:

"In all the best public houses, whether Gin Palace, coaching inn or wayside beerhouse, the façade is of immense importance. The Gin Palace front is vulgarly scrolled, with something of the quality of a well-engrossed solicitor's document with its unreadable decorative script, awkward parchment surface and heavily embossed sealing wax stamp. To parallel these the good Gin Palace has a lot of false unstructural ornament and heavy outside hanging lamp, as unfunctional as gaudy necklaces and ear-rings, but how becoming! The best coaching inns have manorial fronts, with the restraint and good proportions of manor houses gone slightly awry. A really good one resembles nothing so much as a manor house 'half seas over'. . . . The desirable appearance of slight drunkenness in façades is obtained in many ways. It may be produced by the simple juxtaposition of bright colours: white squared stucco corners on an orange brick gable, or black or Venetian red or pink corners on a white or pale yellow gable.''

Dimly comprehending this, successful licensees, as distinct from Brewers, have built up a conventional sign language whereby each contrives to indicate that his is a pub which someone cares enough about to dress it up with bits and pieces, by night fairy lights, and by day hanging baskets of flowers, window boxes, shrubs in tubs, garden benches, umbrellas, cart wheels, Dutch blinds. Some degenerated into a sort of Peter Pan grotto with whimsical gnomes, toadstools, or even a yellow painted stage coach. All these efforts represent a sensible commercial attitude. The customer feels, often rightly, that he will be well received and looked after in a place on which such care and thought has been lavished. Conversely, far too many houses, for lack of a wash down every few weeks and a coat of paint every few years give a contrary impression. This, if you do go in, may well turn out to have been misleading.

However, as G. K. Chesterton acknowledged in *The Flying Inn*, and W. D. Shepherd insisted in his section of Allied Breweries' *Exteriors Manual*, the most important single identifying component of any pub exterior is surely the pub sign, preferably pictorial, suspended on a bracket or raised on a post. Next in importance is certainly the pub name, in strong, noticeable lettering across the face of the house. The Brewer's name, as I have hinted above, is of less importance except in places where there is a marked local preference for one Brewer's beer. The *cognoscenti* can in any case often deduce the ownership from many small indications.

The untrained 'designer', especially if he is accustomed to marketing attitudes, is apt to forget that it is not enough just to draw attention to a house. Of course, this must be done first: but what follows? If the eye, once induced to look in a certain direction, is then instantly repelled by what it sees, the whole intention is frustrated. A pub is entitled to draw attention to itself by eccentric design or even grotesquerie, but brash or ignorant treatment, with signs of garish colours cutting across the architectural features, will lower the tone towards that of the bingo parlour. The showing off can be done happily, much as a man does who wears a button-hole and a silver topped cane (or their present-day equivalents). It should be smart; it may be dressy; but it need not be *flash*.

The choice of lettering is relatively easy. The first requirement is that it should have impact and be legible. Secondly it must have 'character', which means guts. Weakness, spideriness, lack of crispness, can make a legend ineffective. A point worth making is that *italic* or *sloping* letters seldom have the same robustness as vertical types; but a strong letter can also be graceful. The appearance must be elegant, but generous, not mean.

One's next concern is to let the customer, once he has made his mind up, find the way in. This does not mean that the entrance must be sited bang in the middle of the main street front. Some customers, because of their motivation to take cover, prefer to enter from a side alley or through a secluded porch, so the fact that a particular crack or inlet leads to the door must be made subtly but sufficiently clear. Emphasis can be given by means of contrasting colour, tone or texture, by projecting canopies or structural hoods, or at night by careful application of tones, colours and arrangements of light. One may be reluctant to walk into total gloom, but if at the end of a short tunnel of darkness a gleam of warm-coloured light can be seen, the man who feels he could do with a pint will find the invitation irresistible.

Whatever devices are used, over-emphasis of the supermarket kind should be avoided. This distinction is similar to that between a clear command and a startling shout. We can expect better results from the former.

Even the beginnings of commercial clutter in the window and on the mullions cannot destroy the quality of such an exterior

Part II

CURRENT INFLUENCES ON THE PUB

1 The Breweries

At least two points made in the foregoing chapters suggest that foresight has not always been the Brewers' strongest point. Collectively they do not seem to have kept their ears close enough to the right bit of ground. Either, having failed to notice the clouds, they complain when it rains that they have no umbrellas, or (to change the metaphor yet again) they dive into deep shelters as the all-clear sounds!

To this generalisation I can remember one splendid exception, Neville G. Thompson, whose brother became the chairman of Allied Breweries. It was on his initiative that Ind Coope and Allsopp built extensive new bottling stores at Burton at precisely the moment they proved to be needed: but even he once told me, in the mid 1950's, that in another ten years' time there would be no draught beer. Then there was another gentleman who was said to have gone with an axe round a furniture store smashing Victorian advertising mirrors. What the space was needed for I never learned, but I expect it was for old files. Who, indeed, can now contemplate without a sinking heart the amount of decorative glass destroyed by nearly all brewery firms in the process of 'modernisation' of pubs between 1930 and 1965?

Roderick Gradidge, architect, whose knowledge of art history surpasses that of most of the rest of us, has pointed out that there is a time-lag of about twenty years between the general acceptance of a style or fashion and its appearance in pubs. This is, of course, in itself, of little consequence, since period style is an irrelevancy in creating an atmosphere for social drinking: but it is a fact that in general the brewers have trusted their architects too little and too late. Mark Girouard, in his *Victorian Pubs,* has shown convincingly that it was in 1899, when the brewers ceased to pump capital into the pubs for redecorating and rebuilding, that the decline of alcohol consumption dates. Despite this, the contribution made to the Trade by the design professions and the building industry remains undervalued to this day.

Nor can we applaud wholeheartedly the brewers' record in repair and maintenance. Too often, for the sake of a short-term profit the shareholders' assets in bricks and mortar have been allowed to decay. To put off essential roof repairs, or defer until next financial year the eradication of dry rot can have nothing but disastrous results. That these things happen is largely due to the attitude of the accountants, who seem unable to grasp the simple fact that a stitch of revenue spent in time saves not £9 but £99,000 of capital in rebuilding.

However, three entries on the credit side (to use their own jargon) must be made in favour of brewery firms, large and small. First, they continue to brew beer in quantity, and who else could do that? Secondly, they shoulder the administrative burden of running tens of thousands of pubs. Thirdly, they are public benefactors in that their return per pound of capital invested is absurdly small in comparison with that of other industries. Journalists and politicians should remember this when they refer to the 'vast profits' made by the brewers. Anyone who doubts that without their involvement we should lose an invaluable social asset is at liberty to look up the figures for himself. Furthermore, as owners the brewers are beset on all sides by regulations and the officials who enforce them, from the Licensing Bench to the Fire Brigade and the Environmental Health Officer. Their budgets carry enormous costs of tax collection on behalf of the public. Yet they continue to subsidise, against their own commercial interest, innumerable isolated village inns and taverns whose profits may be marginal or non-existent. None of these considerations should be forgotten by those who, like myself, are frequently exasperated by Brewers' perversity and lack of response.

2 Other Owners Of Pubs

Pubs not owned by Breweries are of two sorts – Free houses and Multiples. The former are popularly supposed to be the cream of the Trade, but like the little girl in the nursery rhyme they are horrid when they are bad. Once in the hand of the wrong owner the pub is at his mercy, and nothing but the sanctions of Local Authority – a dubious ally – or Licensing Bench is able to restrain him from ill-considered alterations or, possibly worse still, destructive neglect. He may want to make a packet quickly and get out, leaving behind him a wreck devastated in three ways – socially, structurally and economically. The Brewers sometimes commit similar errors, but at least they have some experience of the business, which he may not. I will not deny that often enough they seem as reluctant to learn from tradition as they are unsuccessful in forecasting trends: but there is a certain 'deposit of faith' handed down, a basic knowledge of what it is all about, which enables them to guide tenants and instruct managers to avoid the worst kinds of excess.

Against this, of course, is the argument that the owner of a Free House, free of Brewery bureaucracy, can keep a grip on the pub and ensure that essential maintenance and care does not go by default, in which matter, as I have suggested above, some Breweries have a poor record. Too many of their tied houses are distantly controlled by charming impractical accountants, remote from day to day problems, unaware of deteriorating fabric and sagging foundations, living in a cloud-cuckoo-land of fantasy. Few of them seem to pay very much attention to their 'service departments', the architects, building surveyors and estate managers. Thus, the responsible and enlightened Free House owner is quite likely to leave them standing. There is also the unworthy suspicion which I have heard expressed, that officials of every kind are less exacting in their dealings with individual owners than with a Brewery, but I would not suggest that inducements to leniency are offered or accepted. A reputable business of good standing could hardly afford to risk such involvement.

Multiples are firms who run chains of pubs, some of them leased from Brewers, but do not themselves brew. Those which are their own property they describe as 'Free'; which may be strictly accurate but is quite misleading, since the pubs have many of the features characteristic of the large organisation. Even those owned by Brewers, though technically Tenanted, have salaried managers in charge and share the characteristics of managed houses. One has the impression that the larger the firm the worse the pubs they control. Once I dreamed of becoming a multiple tenant with only six pubs, relieving the manager of each on one day a week. Whether this would work financially I do not know, but it can be said that some firms with more than six houses can produce better results in terms of customer-appeal than many brewery managed houses. On the other hand, it has been known for a pub reverting from multiple to brewery control to be found in a state of vile disrepair. It depends on the firm. Unfortunately, Breweries cannot just pay their money and take their choice. They are subject to an operation which somewhat resembles blackmail. A multiple will offer a conditional tie in a number of pubs which are their own property in return for tenancy of one which is not.

There are faults on both sides, but there may be a lesson to be learned from at any rate one multiple. Periodic inspections, or Captain's Rounds, are held in every house in rotation. In this way, not only does the Director become more closely acquainted with all his houses, but the licensee cannot get away with the kind of villainy quite often revealed when, for the first time in several years, a brewery official finds the time to walk upstairs. It is true that the man in the bar is not directly affected by the families camping out in the disused Clubroom, or by the dog-droppings of years which entirely cover the second floor: but would not all of us be happier if the perpetrators of such malpractice were quickly rumbled and drummed out of the Trade? The smaller the number of pubs controlled the better the chance of this happening. Conversely, of course, too few houses per Director would mean either a fall in profits or a rise in the price of beer!

3 The Licensee, His Wife And His Staff

One can imagine a pub which, other things being equal, would be ideal for everyday use, and I would urge those responsible to think about it: a labyrinth of loosely connected interior spaces, intersected by see-through partitions, equipped with alcoves and changes of level in floor and ceiling, indeterminate in plan shape; enclosed in warm-coloured, well rubbed, semi-lustrous surfaces, mostly of natural materials and gleaming glass; linked with the great outdoors by fleeting glimpses of the street or countryside; having pools of glowing light in mellow surroundings; not over-furnished, the tables, stools and benches of strong timber subtly formed, burnished by contact with generations of arse and elbow; fitted with a modest counter having a polished and moulded hardwood top.

But other things are not equal. Normally the choice of a pub is made by means of a consensus among one's drinking friends. I have even found myself obliged, after much resistance, to move from a local whose only real fault was the sourness and rudeness of the licensee's wife. My friends, and many others, just refused to put up with her, and so the whole loosely-knit agglomeration of drinking schools, composed of half a dozen overlapping groups of four or five members each, deserted the house and assembled in another pub just down the road. This second pub was picked from three or four other possibles within easy walking distance mainly because the beer was acceptable, but even this would have been insufficient if the faces behind the counter had been severe or surly. From this I conclude that the ideal pub is the one with the ideal licensee, if female, or licensee's wife! To do them justice the Brewers are fully aware of this aspect, and a lot of thought is given to the appointment of every licensee, whether manager or tenant, nor do they forget the all-important wife.

A pub manager receives a salary, and the Brewery takes both wholesale and retail profit: but a tenant, having paid to the brewery a rent and bought from it his stock, makes what he can. The Manager may or may not be given a franchise for the catering only, and run it as a business of his own, paying for this privilege a sum which also covers the use of any catering equipment

94

which the Brewery may install. Apart from his annual bonus, and the profits of the catering if any, he has no financial incentive to increase the 'wet' trade of the house or to contribute his individual touches to the pub's character. This may be why managed houses are sometimes criticised as being soulless, impersonal places – a sweeping generalisation which I cannot support. It is, however, true that, more often than tenancies, they seem to fall into a dismal state of dirt and neglect. A determined Tenant is better able to take the notional risk of spending money on cleaning and furnishing, despite the vacillations of the accountants. By going it alone he stands a good chance of reversing a downward spiral. A manager can only be dragged down in to the whirlpool, knowing all the time that he will be blamed for others' neglect.

The Tenant's situation is more complicated, and there are three ways of looking at his relationship with the Brewer, the landlord: his own, the Brewers', and the customers'. Here I am concerned chiefly with the third, which is itself double-sided. Either, by lack of encouragement, the Brewery will prevent the Tenant from realising the pub's full potential; or conversely it may restrain him, by wise guidance, from making undesirable transformations. Both these things happen. Everything depends upon the individuals concerned on both sides of the Agreement. Inevitably my own feeling is that Tenants in general should pay more attention to the Brewery's ideas, which are based on a wealth of experience and knowledge. It is fallacious, for example, to claim that because a Tenant pays for the furnishings he should have an unfettered voice in their selection. In fact, he is only lending the money, and whenever he leaves he will receive a fair valuation from the ingoing Tenant. In the meantime it is not only his trade but the Brewer's which will suffer if wrong choices are made. It is surely reasonable, therefore, that these should be the subject of discussion with the Brewery's professional staff. Collectively they must have more experience, and possibly more flair, than any average licensee is likely to have been able to gain in a lifetime.

The comparison could be summed up by saying that if Managers do not always make sufficient contribution to the look of the pub, some tenants need to be guided by the landlord to ensure that their innovations are neither overdone nor misconceived. If everyone concerned were as capable as the best on all three sides, the problems in both types of houses would, *ipso facto*, evaporate. My present contribution is aimed at helping all three, and if only they will listen I shall be well satisfied.

Almost as important as the Licensee and his wife is the bar staff he employs. How enlightened is the Tenant who, by means which are no business of mine, attracts and keeps the services of those whose efficiency, appearance and demeanour have the right impact on customers. Nor, when I say 'appearance', do I mean 'sex'. One often hears it said, with a nudge and a smirk, that busty barmaids do more good for the trade than any amount of atmosphere, or (even) than a perfect pint. Be that as it may, I must confess to a personal prejudice against them. There is plenty of time for such indulgence outside Permitted Hours! Am I the only one who, having gone to the pub to

95

drink and converse, finds any strong distraction from these objectives offensive? In any case, if sex you must have, does the late lamented motherly barmaid's vast bosom in black satin not convey a more direct association with the idea of drinking than any pretty poppet with a pert posterior?

Possibly the first requirement in a barmaid or barman is that she/he should enjoy her/his work. An equable temperament is basic to the task. Too much hearty laughter can be as badly out of place as a morose countenance, and a skilful operator will judge and adjust himself to the mood of his customers, conversing with the talkative and respecting the privacy of the introspective. Worst of all bar people is the avid reader, who, at a slack time, returns to his paper-back or comic after serving a lone customer. Attributes which are (or should be) taken for granted are speed, efficiency and a quick eye for an empty glass: but none of these are of much use if they are accompanied by a stern look on a straight face. Nor should it be forgotten that a genial rudeness is always preferable to false deference.

The way the staff dress also has its importance. Black coats and striped trousers are much too formal, white jackets too clinical. Even plum-coloured uniform, though it blends more comfortably into a sociable atmophere, can introduce a whiff of the institution, emphasising the pub's connection with an impersonal and distant organisation. The Marketing fraternity may think this desirable, but the customers don't. They know very well that the barmen (in Managed pubs) are paid by the Brewery, but they feel in their bones that this is not an aspect of the trade which ought to be stressed. It runs against the feel of the place as the licensee's home, and thus detracts from the quality of welcome they rightly demand.

It's always a sign of a good pub when bar staff are found using the house in their off-duty hours. Could one describe as 'collegiate' the atmosphere in such a pub? A community has grown up between those serving and those served in such a way that they can intermingle unselfconsciously, and their roles are partly interchangeable. It is not unknown for one or two specific regulars to be allowed and expected to step in and serve if the licensee, being for the moment without other staff, is called away to the telephone, or to attend to an unexpected delivery.

As to whether or not one should buy drinks for bar-people, I know of only one rule, which is to do so only if I feel warm-hearted towards them (and even then, not every day) – otherwise not. Adherence to this suggestion would mean that the better ones were best rewarded. However there is one character I for one will never treat – the one who comes out from behind the counter of his own volition and plays the juke box. The Licensee, of course, may do as he pleases, and if I don't like him I must go elsewhere: nor am I referring to the barman whom the licensee for any reason has instructed to put coins in the machine. No, my objection is confined to the paid member of staff who chooses, for his own pleasure and entertainment, to override the preference of all the paying customers present, a preference they have clearly expressed by not paying for the music.

4 The Law And Various Regulations

No matter how irksome they may seem from time to time in any good drinking man's life, the restrictions of the English law have played their part in the development of the Pub through history. They have produced a system which expresses the genius of our people, on both sides of the counter, and this is threatened by those who would precipitately alter the law. There is a danger that the delicate balance which has been achieved may be inadvertently destroyed, with the loss of many excellent pubs and, in those that remain, of precisely those qualities which are envied throughout the world, and which we all enjoy.

'Permitted Hours' are an example. At present 'alcohol' may be legally bought and consumed in London pubs for nine hours each weekday. Let us consider some results which would follow if this were extended to allow, not the extreme provision of twenty-four hours, but only, say, eighteen, from 7.00 am until 1.00 am the next day.

First, a lot of pubs would be unable to meet the shift-staffing requirements. They would be driven out of business by those which could. The likelihood is that only a preponderance of large managed houses in densely populated areas would survive. What would become of our much-loved little locals in villages and in outer-urban back streets? Already many of the latter type find it impractical to open all the hours they are at present allowed. They defer opening until 7.00 pm, especially on Saturday nights. Others, in the country, start their lunchtime session about an hour late. What is the sense of demanding extra hours when some find the present latitude more than they need?

Furthermore the price of drinks would be sure to escalate to prohibitive levels. In Holland, where bars are open all day until 1.00 am, the prices are, by British standards, alarmingly high; and it is worth noting that in the afternoon between 3.00 pm and 6.00 pm very little drinking appears to be done. All the lights and heating are going full blast, and staff must remain on duty, for the sake of two or three old ladies consuming coffee and pastries. Are we not better off in this country where other establishments cater for this need, and we can still afford a few pints when the ordinary man's working day brings the opportunity to relax on the way home?

Again, with extended hours, licensees would be forced by economic pressure to introduce all sorts of extraneous gimmicks and distractions in order to pay the fuel and wages bills incurred in slack periods, and so the proper character of the pub would be eroded.

Yet again, there is little doubt that extended hours would lead to all the evils of excessive drinking. It is precisely in the smaller pubs which would be threatened that kindly restraint can most easily and effectively be applied by licensees to discourage over-indulgence. The call of 'Time' is always a salutary reminder of our personal responsibilities! Let every social drinker ask himself, and give an honest answer to the question, "How often, in the morning, do you reflect that it is just as well that last night's 'closing time' induced you to go home?"

Children in Pubs

There is no doubt that the law relating to the admission and conduct of young people in licensed premises (excluding clubs) is in an incomprehensible tangle. More than once even the licensed trade newspaper, *The Morning Advertiser*, has had to correct itself after making a considered pronouncement, thus leaving confusion worse confounded. Nevertheless, I am wholly convinced that the unrestricted admission of children into pubs would be a disaster. By all means let there be rooms where parents may take their offspring, and of course they must be allowed to drink while the children are there. My own view is that children over fourteen should be allowed to have a drink also while their parents are there. That way the youngsters would be taught an acceptable 'way of drinking', and some of the excesses committed by those who are (or can persuade a Licensee that they are) over eighteen might be eliminated. But such a room requires supervision, which implies a hole in the wall, and that might be regarded as a counter, which would make the room a bar and (as the law seems to be at present) automatically exclude the children. Clearly it would be uneconomical to provide waiter service in all such rooms. Possibly the answer is a window fixed closed, the parents fetching their drinks from a nearby dispense point outside the room. But whatever the powers that be in their wisdom decide, let us not have the bars themselves invaded by kids. The pressure to permit this is mounting, and already certain otherwise well run pubs are admitting toddlers in defiance of the law. I have even seen a little girl sitting on a tall stool at the counter, sucking Coke through a straw. There are never enough tall stools for the real drinkers anyway! But the main objection to the admission of infants must be that most of the rest of us don't want them there. Our own, no less than other people's children are one of the things we come in to get away from. Their shrill voices and their occasional outbursts of tears, even their happy high-pitched laughter, can destroy the conversation and companionship of friends, the taste of the beer, and the atmosphere of the whole, quiet, enjoyable session. Therefore

98

it is important that provision should be made for parties of mixed ages within the *pub*, but not, please not, in the bar.

The teenage tribe are, of course, another matter, and I have no intention of sticking my neck out on the question of the precise age at which they should first be allowed, unaccompanied, to have a beer in the bar. In any case, is it not improper that young people should be segregated, spoken of and dealt with separately, driving them perhaps into antagonistic attitudes, or even slowing the rate of their natural development? An ideal situation is the bar where adult people of all ages happily mingle, and mutual restraint is exercised. This is good social training. Older people sometimes appear to forget that youngsters are human: they should remember Mr Pitt's retort to the monarch, for nothing is more certain than that time will amend youth. The younger they are the more they will look for innovation and change, but nothing we may contrive in order to cater for such fleeting taste will last more than a year. Something still newer will then be sought by those who have recently arrived at the lower end of the permitted age-scale, and further transformation will be needed to keep up with demand. Therefore it is a total fallacy to suppose that any special appeal should be made to the young. They are well able to enjoy and appreciate a timeless social drinking atmosphere as described in this book. Often it is the oldest pubs which are frequented by a young clientele. They are not so stupid as some people with a gimmick to sell would have us think.

Women in Pubs

The sole effect on one Brewery's London estate of the Sex Discrimination Act, was that two Ladies' Only bars had to be re-labelled; with the surely quite unintended result that a few respectable old dears, who used to enjoy a Guinness-and-gossip away from the men-folk, were exposed to the unwelcome intrusion of males into their sanctum.

Why, indeed, should a pub not offer, where the demand exists, opportunity for either sex to escape, for a brief space, from the company of the other? Such a respite from one, at least, of the stresses of life is beneficial rather than harmful to anyone. No-one, I think, would wish to return to the days when women frequenting pubs were automatically regarded as being of easy virtue. In Scotland within living memory it was socially unacceptable for a man and his wife to have a drink together in public except in a hotel bar. Such a state of affairs was deplorable. Nevertheless, in my view, we are now becoming too rigid in the opposite direction. Perhaps women should be allowed to have a little bar to themselves if they so wish, and by the same rule so should the men.

What I do contest is the doctrine that bars should be in some way altered or restyled in order to appeal to women. For a start, the average male pub-designer seems to have little idea what does appeal to them. The general notion seems to be that they want something respectable, smooth, soft or 'ladylike'. What rubbish is this! The best female pub-designers, whose work I applaud, know better. When, in the early 20th century, women began to invade the pub, they liked it as it was, and a large part of its appeal to them was precisely that it had, in fact, a strongly masculine character. I suspect that the likely result of making a specifically 'feminine' bar would be that pretty soon it would be full of male homosexuals. (Why not? They are as much entitled to a social drink as the rest of us. All I am saying is that a 'feminine' bar will not appeal to the ladies.)

On one thing, however, women do insist, and that is a decent lavatory. Men will put up with almost anything except a vile stink, whether of drains or of perfumed disinfectant, but women, unless they have a bit of comfort in the loo, will veto visits and decline invitations to a particular pub.

Proliferation of Licences

The selling of alcoholic drink is a specialist's job, since its consumption is patently capable of abuse. In the past Licensing Magistrates have been strict in ensuring that it is sold only by suitable people in suitable places. No doubt errors have been made, but in general it is true to say that until recent years excesses were thereby kept in check and the beneficial nature of the Trade preserved. However there is now much concern about increased drinking by youngsters. Who can doubt that this trend is due to the ease with which they can obtain bottles from the supermarket?

Regulations (Planning, Building and Public Health)

Often it seems to anyone involved in the Licensed Trade that our pubs are beset by a regiment of jackbooted antagonists, brandishing Books of Regulations and intent on the extermination of our human, sociable business; and it is a fact that the impact of officialdom on your friendly neighbourhood local is out of all proportion to its potential for harm. Indeed, it is the question of proportion which deserves attention by the authorities. Most of those entrusted with the enforcement of rules designed to protect the public are sincere in their desire to do so, but it is difficult for them to avoid giving an opposite impression. Any proposal to form a little hole in an internal wall the better to serve a little-used Smoke Room, and to widen a gap in the hedge for customers' cars to gain access to the yard, is likely to involve the Licensing Bench, the District Surveyor, the Planning Officer, the Fire Prevention Officer, and the Environmental Health Officer. All these officers, once official attention is drawn to the house, may well be joined by those concerned with music and dancing, provision for the disabled, and water supply. Hard on their heels may come the Conservation Society and the Performing Rights people. Regulars like the VAT-man, the Weights and Measures, the Excise and the village bobby may find themselves crowded out of the Snug.

Consider, if you will, the effect of applying to a decent little pub with two bars the Environmental Health requirements intended to regulate the conduct of a banqueting suite, or to ward off squalor in the Turkish Takeaway, (which cannot, as the pub can, be controlled by other means). Double-bowl sinks and wash-hand-basins crowd out the stock. Impervious surfaces (which generally means plastic) seem more appropriate to milk shakes than to beer. Kitchen-type finishes which, in a restaurant, could be kept off-stage, obtrude and give offence in a bar. Many years ago a Sanitary Inspector (*sic*) of laudable percipience remarked that beer is a fine germicide, and it is a pity that this is not always remembered, even if it is known. What will be the reaction of an over-protected public when they have been deprived of the last honest oak counter top? Can anyone pretend that a pile of steaming sausages has the same appeal in a glass case? It is indeed to the credit of our officials' common-sense that the regulations are not in every case rigorously applied: but they could be, and they are wrong. Can our MPs and Civil Servants not grasp the fact that an organism such as the human body can develop no resistance to infection if it is never, from cradle to early grave, exposed to any? (or so my doctor assures me).

In pubs where there is Entertainment matters become worse. To meet the Fire Regulations, repellently plain doors have often replaced beautifully moulded two-inch thick mahogany ones, because the area of Edwardian brilliant-cut glass in them was 'excessive' – that is, larger than a moderately-sized peephole. Unsightly lobbies and screens designed to give 'compartmentation' obstruct both supervision and circulation. Even a short flight of steps may be regarded as a staircase which has to be 'enclosed'. Intriguing views in a labyrinthine series of bars are visually blocked, and thus much of one's pleasure in the spatial qualities of a building may be done away with. All this is the result of trying to make the same regulations, desirable in a theatre, fit the rather different case where, for a couple of hours in the evening, a little group of musicians offers a bit of cheerful sound to the occupants of a bar, no matter how small it is or how few they are. It is like trying to fit a dog with a horseshoe, and it is high time Parliament gave some respite to the hapless officials entrusted with so absurd a task.

Lavatories present a similar problem. Of course they have their importance. Not for nothing is a bibulous occasion referred to as a piss-up, and a talented performer at the bar as a piss-artist! In the immortal words of T. E. B. Clarke in *What's Yours?*, "beer drinking is an exercise which would prevent [the Guv'nor] from continuing to apply himself assiduously to his work, causing, as it does, frequent tiresome interruptions". This applies to the customers, too, even if our task is merely the assiduous enjoyment of a few more jars. Is this not, in fact, one reason for an increased consumption of short drinks by those whose advancing years have reduced the elasticity of the personal hydraulic system?

But having made this acknowledgement, I must now state my belief that the floor-space and the funds devoted to lavatory accommodation has been grossly and unnecessarily inflated over the years. Even at closing time it is rare to find queues in the Gents. (The Ladies may be another matter, but I doubt it). Local Authorities, aided and abetted by Licensing Benches, insist upon a scale of provision which, in a theatre or concert hall, might be desirable when everyone goes dashing out at the end of the performance;

101

but in a pub this prodigality is out of place, because one is free at any time briefly to interrupt the conversation. Concentrated peak demand does not arise.

From a pub owner's point of view a lavatory is non-productive. It occupies valuable covered floor space which could otherwise be producing a profit. The architect's job in keeping the cost per square metre of drinking area down to a viable level is difficult enough without his being forced to plan for large spaces which will be unoccupied for a great part of the time: and this dilemma is exacerbated when the official requirement is for highly costly wall finishes. The main requirement to the customer is that a lavatory should be clean, and I know many drinkers who prefer a spotless dado of tar surmounted by freshly whitewashed brick to any amount of smelly and grimy porcelain or glazed tiles. Environmental Health Officers should remember that, no matter how easy to clean a surface may be, it is sure to become and remain filthy if the will to clean it does not exist. Unfortunately, the accountants' attitude once again baffles common-sense. They would rather spend capital on expensive wall tiles than revenue on wages and whitewash.* Admittedly the root cause of this appears to be in the system of tax, and I suggest that someone should put his mind to its amendment.

In country pubs, who except the Health Officer is really offended by the fact that the lavatory is 'outside'? Not, I think, anyway, the male customers. Even on a wet and windy night a brief excursion across the yard never hurt anyone, provided that there is a bit of a roof when you get there.

---

* The decoration of lavatories deserves a little attention. I do not go along with the venerable brewery director, long since retired, who forbade the use of any colours but black and white. This may be ideal in particular cases, but I have never doubted the truth of the maxim that women like a bit of pink in the loo! Nor should one forget that, as Roderick Gradidge first pointed out, the colour treatment even of the Gents can affect the continuity of the evening. To walk from a cosy bar into a lavatory all painted white and brilliantly lit can induce a mild sense of shock. It may even be disturbing enough to cause one to leave and go home at an unwontedly early hour.

5 Food And Entertainment

When is a drinking place not a pub? Apart from certain peripheral cases mentioned earlier, the answer, to the customer, is pretty clear. It is that in any bar where social drinking takes second place the full requirement is not met. That is to say, not that other activities are always out of place, but rather that if they are allowed to *predominate* the result will be something less, or at any rate something other, than a pub.

Entertainment and food are the two most common intruders. Certainly there is room for both in varying degrees in almost all pubs everywhere, but it is when they begin to take over from the drinking, or to destroy sociability, that true Pub value is lost. There are, unhappily, plenty of pubs with so little merit that their complete or partial transformation into eating or entertainment places would show a net gain to the public at large, as well as to the owners. However, I do suggest that we should guard against this happening in pubs which are already good of their kind.

The trouble with loud modern entertainment is that it is not really sociable. One cannot converse, and conversation is an essential part of social drinking. Furthermore, entertainment does not always bring in to a pub the anticipated additional trade. In the early 1970's a series of power cuts well demonstrated this point. I then heard of three houses in London, two managed and one tenanted, where the licensees were obliged by lack of power for their amplification equipment to cancel entertainment for the duration of the cuts. In all three the trade lost amounted to less than the saving on artistes' fees, so that without entertainment better profit was gained. It may not always be true to say that any licensee who has to resort to music in order to bring in trade is thereby admitting failure. It may be the designer who has failed. In all three cases I have mentioned the bars had been fairly recently re-designed by a first-rate pub architect, but no-one had appreciated the pulling power of the environment he had created.

'Food' is hardly a precise term, and since the point I am making is a matter of degree it may be thought necessary to consider the different levels of catering which may be provided: but in fact it is not the style of the food

103

which is significant in this context so much as the way in which it is presented, its extent in relation to the total licensed floor area, and still more its layout. An inn such as the White Hart, St Albans, could support an excellent restaurant at least equal in area to the sum of the two bars, partly because it was separated from them by an entrance hall, and did not impinge upon the consciousness of the drinkers. At the other extreme, I have known stalwart customers permanently offended (and therefore lost) by the volume of cottage pie and beans being passed over their heads while they waited with decreasing patience to be served with their gins and tonics. Even if a snack counter is separate on the other side of the room, it can exasperate the man who comes in for a pint when he finds three people busily serving food while a single barman tries unsuccessfully to cope with nearly twenty metres of drinking counter. Nor is it only a matter of speed of service. Equally off-putting to the drinker is the battery of hot and cold food cabinets on the counter, and the tables laid with white table-cloths. It is better to make your restaurant look like a bar than vice-versa – a fact which seems to have been understood by the operators of Berni or Schooner Inn type catering, whatever one may think about their style of 'decor'. None the less, I fear that these and others like them must be classed as non-pubs. The great merits they have are not those of a pub, and it is only a pity that so many formerly good pubs have been lost in such transformations. Almost any building, old or new, could have been internally reconstructed to provide a catering place of this type.

Mainly in the north at present there is a thing called a 'Vittle Inn', described as "Not a restaurant, but much more than a pub", and as a type of eating bar these deserve special mention. Undoubtedly the emphasis is on the food, but the design provides so excellent a drinking atmosphere that at first one is hardly aware of what it is the place has that is "more than a pub". The most noticeable difference is that the drinks counter is considerably shorter than one would expect in a true drinking bar. The style is traditional but, except for a few ornaments, it is entirely 20th century – a modern bar interior entirely recognisable as a Pub, and so successfully carried out that it should be emulated by designers elsewhere. What I do not understand is why the owners do not realise what their architects* have done. The advertising blurb issued at the inception of these 'Inns' states, "The benches, tables, beams and period bric-a-brac put you right back in the 18th century". In fact, they do not, but they are a fine example of the meaning of the word 'continuity' in pub design. Only two things are perhaps to be regretted – that the waitresses are dressed up in irrelevant 'period' costume, and that the bars' appearance has been developed in places mainly for eating. Like wine bars, they look more like pubs than the real thing very often does in our times.

* Fergus H. Frost and his staff and successors at Tetleys.

6 The Good News

As we move into the 1980's some of the influences I have mentioned do appear to threaten the smooth development of our pubs, but fortunately there are as well a number of more encouraging signs. The Brontosaurus Brewery (35 tons of body with 1 lb of brain) is dead, and we now hear that small is again beautiful. The policy makers are reacting to the demand for a more natural and traditional image in the whole social drinking scene as they did to the shift towards cask-conditioned beer. Undoubtedly the two trends are linked. Be it noted that the influences which resulted in the softening of pubs and the virtual disappearance of the Public Bar in some areas came, not from architects, but from other sources. Even those of us who accepted the modern rejected the modernised, and at all times we resisted the flood of carpet. We applaud the move to wood from plastic, and we are happy to see an increased awareness of the fact that it can pay to restore the best old pubs. I would be happier still if I could see more evidence that this is matched by a desire to conserve the *components* which are best in all old pubs. Still, the prospect is far from desperate. On the whole, and despite the loss of many of the finest and least pretentious interiors over the last 30 years, there are surely fewer really ghastly drinking places to be found.

If it is true, as I have suggested, that everything we, the drinking public, like about the Pub has resulted from a process of uninterrupted gradual change it must be in the commercial interest of pub owners to resist sudden upheavals, and to test each projected innovation against the five general and universal principles I have described. We must insist that the Pub continues to reject whatever is incompatible with its nature and to hive off into other establishments any actual or contemplated use which conflicts with an incomparable tradition. As long as the owners continue to realise and to value the unique quality of the licensed Trade, and as long as customers are bloody-minded enough to turn down whatever they don't really like, we shall continue to enjoy our enviable Way Of Drinking.

Part III

REVIVAL OF
THE FITTEST

1 The King

'The King' is a market pub in a small but thriving Yorkshire industrial town. It was built in the early 19th century, and 'modernised' between the two Wars. During the 1950's it received a refurbishing, and the large, rambling lounge is not in too bad a state, but the smaller Public Bar has been allowed to go down. A room about 13.5 × 4.5 m, it is a simple rectangle on plan; albeit the plainness is somewhat alleviated by the fact that it was formerly two rooms, one three times as long as the width of the other, and what remains of the dividing wall, above and at each end of the new opening, forms a visual break. Also there are two intruding entrance lobbies, one of them on the short splay at the street corner. The servery, about half the length of the room, projects from the inner wall, and over it is a solid plastered canopy 400 mm deep. The underside of the opening between the two parts of the room is 15 mm higher than that of the canopy, and the ceiling height generally is approximately 2.5 m.

At present the ceiling is a drab khaki-ish green, and the walls of slightly textured plaster are painted from top to bottom in pale cream. The floor is of grey thermoplastic tiles, and the fixed seating which runs along most of the walls is covered with dark plum-coloured leathercloth in a reasonably good state of repair. The counter top is of 'oak veneer' laminate, but the front, evidently built in the 1920's or early 30's, is the best thing in the room, being splendidly panelled in polished hardwood. The curtains are in plain orangey-red.

There is one very sub-standard low circular table with a cream laminate top, and six fine rectangular cast-iron tables to the tops of which the same repellent material has been applied. A few solid wooden stools, the tops upholstered with leathercloth to match the seating, complete the loose furniture. On the walls hang one small oval mirror, one picture, several notices, two fire-arms and a juke-box remote-control cabinet. The backfitting is a good, practical, solid affair, with no frills, but an unscreened fluorescent tube in the top of it glares into one's eyes. A simple timber potshelf is suspended from the canopy by black metal rods.

108

All the six pendant lights in the public space are white acrylic cylinders about 120 mm diameter and 200 mm deep, suspended 2.25 m above floor level, and in the servery are seven similar fittings hung close under the false ceiling behind the canopy. The room is thus quite adequately but too evenly lit.

Certainly this is a bar which has seen better days, and our job is simply to ensure that it sees a good many more in the future. This will necessarily entail turning back the clock to some small extent, but it would be absurd to attempt the creation of an early Victorian Tap from such a point of departure. All we need is an unpretentious pint-drinking place in which the market workers and other customers can feel that their requirements are being met with sympathy and understanding.

First, let us try to make the place a bit more human, a bit less like the inside of a cardboard shoe-box. It definitely needs a frieze, and also a dado to give additional horizontal emphasis and to fill in the uneasy gaps of pale wall between the lengths of seating. It is tempting to suggest abolition of the crude and heavy canopy which, with its potshelf, tends to segregate the staff away from the customers: but the making good after such an operation would be grossly expensive. The improvements, after all, must *pay*. Fortunately we can get the best of both worlds by running the timber rail at the base of our proposed frieze right round the front of the canopy as well, so that when we have painted different colours above it and below the appearance of it will be less ponderous. This, together with the provision of three large framed mirrors on the largest vacant areas of wall, and with adjustments to the lighting, should suffice for spatial treatment.

The most offensive surface in the room is the laminate top of the counter, and it will be well worth while to fix a new solid hardwood top 25 mm thick straight down on to the existing top, which will still give an acceptable elbow height. Like most counters of the period this one is 3ft 6in high, but 3ft 7½in (say 1100 mm) is marginally more comfortable to the average male perpendicular drinker. The front edge will be moulded, and a further timber moulding will be fitted underneath to mask the existing laminate upstand. Because of the textured surface, ceiling and walls will have to be painted, and the simpler the scheme the better. A light tan ceiling and a peat coloured dado with sand colour between will provide an unobtrusive background for the main activities of the bar – chatter about sport and about the market, and the sinking of pints. The floor, of course, will be 'Rosewood' lino – obligatory in all such bars unless an acceptable permanent floor exists already.

The fixed seating would have been better in a warm golden-brown, but in view of the cost of upholstery and the fact that there is not too much red in proportion we shall have to be content to make the few minor repairs needed and revive the woodwork. However the stools are in a tatty state and these can be re-covered in brown. The little circular table may serve some purpose in the licensee's flat, and we shall replace it with a new Britannia. The rectangular tables will require new hardwood tops, with rounded corners and the indispensable moulded nosing. In addition to the mirrors already mentioned we shall need a few extras to fill in blank areas of wall space – a large noticeboard of green felt in a plain frame, a number of framed prints in monochrome, possibly of local scenes, and a couple of maps having some relevance to the district, might well serve. As for the curtains, this is just the sort of bar where they are not needed at all.

Quite a lot of dominoes is played here of an evening, so it is essential to illuminate the particular table tops pretty intensely. To avoid an uncomfortable glare for the rest of the customers, whose eyes are not directed downwards, this can be achieved by means of cylindrical downlighters, matt black inside and out, fixed to the ceiling and fitted with internally silvered spot lamps. One of these should be sufficient over each dominoes table. For general light we must find some ceiling fittings (or pendants hung on short cables) with translucent, though *not* transparent, amber coloured glass shades, with holes in the bottom giving a cut-off angle of vision steep enough to conceal the lamp from sitting or standing eye levels. The lights behind the counter could be short downlighters fitted with amber perspex skirts to present a warm glow to the observer as well as sufficient plain light downwards on to the counter. Three similar fittings could replace the glaring fluorescent tube in the backfitting.

When the job is completed the result, as in all design work, will represent the effect of a number of careful and accurate choices: in this bar it is unlikely that more than two or three of these will ever be really noticed by anyone; and it is probably true to say that the less we make the drinking man aware that changes have been made the less likely he will be to react unfavourably. After a few weeks let us hope that one of the regulars will say (surprised-like), "Bloody place seems to be gettting bloody crowded these bloody days".

2 The Oak

'The Oak' is a modest, unpretentious pub in a quiet urban side street, at the end of a mid-Victorian terrace of two-storey houses. At present it is your true 'local', having no casual trade, though at evening rush hour a few back-doubling motor commuters do drive through the street.

Excluding a single-storey lavatory extension at the rear the pub is approximately 7 m². The Public, entered by the front door, is L-shaped, the toe of the L leading back towards the Ladies' and Gents' entrances. The servery, too, is L-shaped, but in the opposite direction, the toe forming a quadrant servery in the little Saloon Bar. Between the Public and the Saloon is a rudimentary off-sales, linked to each by a door opening in a low timber screen and in a wall, respectively, and giving access to the minor side street by another door. This tiny area is now used for drinking, but accommodates at most two people against the counter. At the rear of the Saloon is one window and at the front, in the Public, there are two, with green and white leaded panes of a 1920-ish pattern. Ceiling height throughout is about 3 m.

Drinking space is thus little more than a U-shaped passage, which is narrowest in the former off-sales, but severely restricted in the Public, where there is an excessive 1.5 m width behind the counter. This has a fine mahogany top with a moulded nosing, and its front consists of some excellent panelling with bolection moulds, all decently brush-grained: it is surmounted by a repulsive wrought-iron potshelf and grille carrying bottles of cordial, playing cards, glasses and 'stuff'. The modern backfitting has a plastic work-top, with simple timber shelves below and plate glass ones above backed by mirrors in plain timber framing.

The ceiling is a uniform nicotine-cream, but the walls show variations which may relate to earlier subdivisions, now removed. At one end of the Public there is an area of brown lincrusta panelling with a frieze over, and the plywood dado is of varying shades and heights. A brown flock paper of vertical pattern predominates in both bars. The off-sales screen is clad with pale oak veneer. A brown and orange carpet has been laid in the Saloon, and the Public Bar floor is covered with red linoleum so carefully washed that no

111

polish remains. The curtains are plain red, but they are seldom drawn except to keep out the horizontal rays of sunshine on a winter morning.

The furniture is a scratch lot, but includes two Britannias (one with a yellowish laminate top) and a solid rectangular wooden table in the 'toe' of the Public Bar, used for crib. Around it stand tall-backed dining chairs which, when pushed back, effectively impede urgent passage to the two lavatories. One good old-fashioned padded bench covered with green leathercloth graces the Public. The Saloon has one splendid Windsor armchair, and some grey plastic stackers like those in the church hall. The tall stools throughout are modern suburban kitchen-type with red tops. The inventory is concluded by a small juke-box, a bandit, and four cigarette machines, two of which reduce much-needed counter length in the off-sales and the Saloon.

Most of the artificial light is provided by wall brackets nearly two metres above floor level, and by chandeliers, all fitted with fancy little tan fabric shades, but a fluorescent strip is fixed to the ceiling above the main servery, and a pale fluorescent haze falls on to the upper shelves of the backfitting from an inverted trough.

As it stands, then, despite the accretions, the Oak is not a bad little pub at all. It suffers from long periods of very slack trade in the course of the week, and to open at the start of evening permitted hours is not considered worth while: nevertheless at peak hours it is packed to the doors, and one obvious improvement would be to push the Public Bar counter back about half a metre. This would automatically eliminate the derisory off-sales, and the extra strip of floor area might produce a few extra barrels a year, as well as added convenience: but such an increase could not justify the cost. To make the alteration pay it would be vital, in addition, to enhance the pub's appeal as well.

Let us suppose that this has been accepted: the partition is down, the counter has been cut and moved back, the services adjusted and the floor made good. What do we do next? Here, at any rate, are a few suggestions.

How about the shape of the space. It is pretty well broken up, but even if it were 500 mm wider it would still appear tall. To correct this we must remove the hideous potshelf and replace it with two short lengths of two-tier mahogany shelves for glasses, not suspended from the ceiling but supported on 50 mm diameter polished brass columns; and we must replace the fluorescent tube with three cylindrical downlighters. A little more complexity is desirable, but there is no room for projecting bays of seating, and in this case neither the cost nor the scale of the building would permit false ceilings or raised floors; so the only device we need here is a number of large framed mirrors (decorated or plain) three or four spaced along the party wall and one in the Saloon.

The existing surfaces are reasonably good, the hard, brown mood of the Public marred only by red curtains and lino, and the rather too elaborate flock paper: so let us dye the curtains to a reddish brown, and the new lino will be 'Rosewood'. It will not be an easy job finding a brown and tan wallpaper of a strong geometrical pattern, and if we fail we can fall back on anaglypta painted mid-tan. If a suitable paper can after all be found it should be treated with transparent emulsion glaze. The ceiling colour we shall repeat, and, having formed a frieze about 500 mm deep, paint it in a shade which splits the difference between the ceiling and wall. The dado can remain, with a walnut stain, but it could be reduced to 1150 mm and provided with a 100 mm wide timber shelf at the top for parking one's pint. Alternatively such a shelf could be fitted above shoulder level. There seems to be no good reason for removing the lincrusta; and all the counter front needs is a touch up and a coat of varnish.

The Saloon Bar carpet is quite acceptable and not too badly worn, so the brown in its colouring could be picked up in the ceiling and frieze, and a burnt orange paper with a small all-overish pattern applied to the walls and then covered with so many framed prints and bits and pieces that it all but disappears. However some additional differentiation is needed; deep green velvet dress curtains for a start, with a generous pelmet, and for the rest we shall depend upon the loose furniture.

The vandalised Britannia will need a new polished mahogany top with a moulded nosing, and the plastic stackers will be banished to the yard. For the time being let us be content with four small tub chairs and as many low stools plus two or three tall ones, all covered with deep green draylon to match the curtains. Later, when the trade has improved, we could think about an L-shaped piece of deep-buttoned seating in the corner.

Furniture for the Public is more difficult. The solid wooden table can stay, and we shall have to search the second-hand shops for two or three more to replace the existing rough stuff. The tall stools must go, and be replaced with reproduction turned-leg saddle-tops. Instead of the awkward dining chairs we need an equal number of plain padded stools with mid-brown leathercloth tops. The old bench can be re-covered to match, and if another similar one can be found, we are in luck. Also, along the wall parallel with the counter, where floor space is too restricted for seating, a narrow padded bottom-rest could be fixed, at a height considerably greater than that of a chair seat, say 700 to 800 mm. For any wall areas still vacant we can provide a notice board, a few sepia photographs suitably framed, or cartoons. It would be a good idea to fit deep beige roller blinds to keep out the sun. Finally, the backfitting could be improved quite cheaply by adding a moulded hardwood nosing to the work top, and polishing the wood to a warmer, walnut shade.

Now for the lighting. All the wall brackets except those where people can walk or stand close to the wall should be lowered about 40 mm. The existing shades are a good colour, but something plainer would be more in keeping. The fluorescents in the backfitting will be replaced with down-lighters, and another could be placed over the crib table. The Saloon deserves a new chandelier of brass, with four 200 mm diameter orange-brown glass shades. We shall also need two or three decorative table lamps on quadrant shelves in the corners of the room, at just above seated shoulder-height; and picture lights could be placed above two of the framed prints selected for their size and elaboration.

There are the bones of the job. Any good tenant will find a hundred ways of enhancing his bars' appeal as time goes on, not least by keeping a good polish on things. Still, now that it looks reasonable we need not be ashamed to get rid of the green glass in the upper panes of the windows and give the commuters an inviting glimpse of the interior. Next time past they may very well stop, and all we have to do then is to open the door and make them welcome!

3 The Case Is Altered

Poor Mrs Minnis was doing her best, but honestly she hadn't a notion. On the death of her husband the brewery had allowed her to keep 'The Case Is Altered', and that is just what she did – she altered it: at any rate she made the Smoke Room into a Lounge – the splendid old Smoke Room which was, in fact, by far the larger of the two rooms in the pub. Being a snob, she spent none of the money he left her on the little Tap Room, so mercifully it remains as it was, quarry tiles, ingle, high-backed settle, cross-legged tables and all. In it she did a fair business with the country lads, and a few discriminating regular callers from the town over the hill. However, the trade in the Lounge went into a steady decline, and now that she has departed we must try to help the new tenant to build it up again.

'The Case Is Altered' stands, appropriately enough, near the top of a hill* on an undulating B road much used by motorists dodging the traffic on the main road to the sea. The Smoke Room is a fairly irregular shape, with a low ceiling and a rectangular bay window facing the south-west. In words it is impossible to state the dimensions of such a room, except by giving the total area which is some 40 m^2. At one time it was lined throughout with dark oak panelling, which Mrs M found gloomy and had stripped out. She left the decorative plaster work of the ceiling and painted it a tasteful duck-egg blue, matt. At the same time pink quilted oilcloth was stuck on to the boarded front of the modest counter, and bird's-eye maple laminate on to the oak top. "It does save so much work", she said. On the wide pine boards of the uneven floor she laid a floral pattern carpet in shades of grey, yellow and blue. Green and gold Regency striped paper was hung to the newly plastered walls. Next, yielding to an importunate salesman, she installed a wrought iron concoction of festoons and frills on the top of a projecting seat capping, and then, not liking its blackness, painted it gilt.

Over the counter was fixed a thatched canopy with bamboo supports,

---

* Case Is Altered equals Casa Alta, the high house. Pubs of this name are generally supposed to have been built or re-named by soldiers returning from the Peninsular War.

and this was later interwoven with plastic hops. The curtains and uphol-stery are in ivory and indigo chintz. The old brick fireplace has been filled in with reeded hardboard painted cream, and in front of this stands an anodised electric fire with artificial logs within which some mechanism gives the effect of a pulsating light. A horse collar and brasses have been hung on the wall, with an assortment of willow pattern and Peter Pan plates. There are little oval tables with splayed legs and light oak-veneered tops, in the 1950's 'contemporary' style, and round them stand reproduction wheel-backed chairs with chintz cushions tied on with tapes. A bench of wany-edged elm provides seating for gnomes, but none ever come in. The chromium-plated table lamp and the reclining chair both look as if they had formerly belonged to a seaside boarding house.

Lighting is also shed from wrought-iron and opal glass fittings fixed to the ceiling, and from carelessly 'adzed' oak wall brackets with spherical clear glass globes and amber candle lamps. Behind the counter the till is illumi-nated by a cold cathode tube.

Now, let us not be downhearted. Although admittedly the place is now suitable only for drinking vermouth and eating scampi from a plastic cradle, most of the mayhem is either superficial or portable, For a start, there is nothing much wrong with the three-dimensional shape of the room, so we can concentrate on the surfaces, contents and lighting. Searching the outhouse we are lucky to find enough of the old oak panelling, stacked in a heap, to allow its reinstatement on possibly two thirds of the walls: let us, then, to carry the best of the plates and a few extras, fit a dark-stained plate shelf at 350 mm below ceiling level, filling in below with panelling say half the way round, and forming a dado with what is left over. The unpanelled wall below the shelf will be painted a deep copper beech leaf colour, semi-gloss, as a background to the bits of brass which will also be increased in number.

The ceiling, being fairly low, and having some agreeably decorative plasterwork, needs only a biscuit-coloured paint, again semi-gloss, and this will be carried down the frieze above the plate shelf. Naturally we shall reinstate the oak counter top, and the boarded front will be brush-grained to a shade between walnut and dark oak. The horrible thatch will be removed, together with the gilded wrought-iron screen. A couple of rows of silver and pewter tankards will be hung from the servery ceiling. Maybe the plastic hops will look nice in the Ladies', but the boarding house chair, and the cushions, curtains and carpet will make a bonfire. The pine boards will be sanded and polished, and red 'Turkey' runners and rugs carefully placed where needed. The new curtains will be deep red velvet, and for the upholstery we shall specify real hide (– hang the expense – there is not a great deal of it; the tenant can just afford it and he can be trusted to exclude vandals from a pub such as this). The gnomes' bench will be put in the garden. To replace the scrapped pieces what could be better than an old monk's bench from a country house sale? With luck the same source might yield some genuine 'cricket' tables at a reasonable price. If not, we could make do with almost any solid timber tables, not less than 700 mm high or more than 700 mm diameter (or square, always provided that, if square, the corners are very slightly rounded). Finally, we must of course restore the fireplace, and in it burn, for preference, real logs.

The lighting is not as difficult as it may at first seem. There are very few ceiling points, and these can be straightforward batten holders fitted with simple card or fabric red shades in the shape of a truncated cone. New wall brackets of brass with identical shades will throw little pools of light on to the panelling, and a few teapot-brown glazed earthenware table lamps with slightly larger amber silk shades will complete the main scheme: unless a convenient corner can be found for a standard lamp with a turned timber shaft and a similar shade. The cold cathode tube must be replaced by an 'architectural' tungsten strip concealed from direct view by a shiny copper pelmet. Possibly, as an extra, we could place here and there on the panelling some old framed county maps, or small original portraits of stern old gentlemen wearing dark suits, illuminated by small picture lights.

In a visual sense, all the room needs now is a vivid but comparatively small splash of billiards-cloth green. This might well be contributed by covering the door behind the counter with green felt, patterned with diagonal rows of upholsters' brass domed tacks.

Now what about your Campari and scampi? Certainly, Sir, if that is what you wish we can provide it, just as courteously as if you ordered (as you probably will) one double Scotch, two VSOP Courvoisier brandies, three pure malts, four pints of Burton in thin glasses, five halves of Skol Special, a Worthington White Shield, or six tankards of black velvet. If (which heaven forbid), you want a Buck's Fizz, we can even do that!

4 The Happy Landlord

This basic little pub is situated in the Home Counties and it is doubly well named, because not only is the licensee happy, he is also truly the landlord – he owns the place. This is a Free House.

Some years ago Gareth Lloyd bought the pub from a brewery. It was on its beam ends, having been a (rather badly) managed house since the last tenant left. It is a tiny place, with a licensed area of less than 40 m² – the type of house which is normally tenanted. Perhaps no-one would have it. It stands in the so-called High Street of a quite unremarkable village, surrounded by agriculture but not very far from the edge of the stockbroker belt. A two-storey cottage, its parts were built at different times during the 17th century. There are two bars, the long, narrow Tap Room nearly twice the size of the Square Parlour which, when in earlier days the pub was an alehouse, used to be a private room. These two bars together form an L-shape, and the servery fills the fourth corner to make a 9 m square plan. Each bar is served through a hole in the wall across a short counter projecting only its own width into the room. The ceiling of the Tap is barely 2 m high, and that of the Parlour not very much more.

When Lloyd arrived he found the place depressingly dirty. The shelves of the servery were sparsely stocked and tatty net curtains hung at the windows. The walls of both rooms were bare except for the dadoes of tongued and grooved boarding. In the Tap Room this was bead-moulded as well and equipped with a wooden seat only 380 mm wide, covered with thin padding under black leathercloth. The Tap Room ceiling, crossed by two black beams, and also the walls above dado level, were painted buttery yellow, the dado itself pale grey. The floor of 6 × 6 in red quarry tiles had been covered in part with thin domestic lino of imitation parquet design, with a couple of black rubber darts mats, though no darts were ever played. (There is not really room.) The furniture comprised a scratch lot of transport café tables with bird's-eye maple laminate tops, and a few padded stools.

Except the ceiling and the counter front, both of which were white,

118

everything in the Parlour was red – wallpaper, curtains, seats, carpet, all in different shades of red and of course in different patterns. Even the laminate table tops were the usual slightly bluish shade of pale strawberry pink. The chairs were rather small modern dining chairs of pale coloured wood.

Both rooms were lit by fluorescent tubes fixed to the ceiling, those in the Tap Room placed close to the beams to avoid damage from the impact of people's heads: but the hazard was small, because the whole of the week's trade amounted at that time to a desperate $1\frac{1}{2}$ converted barrels. Now it is nearly twelve, and at an intermediate stage when Gareth had yet to deal with the loose furniture it was already more than ten. Of course it is the personality of the man and his wife which has contributed most to this startling rise, but it may be worth while looking at the detail of what they have done.

First they gave the whole place a determined wash down from top to bottom, ceiling, walls, floor and all the fixtures. They shampooed the carpet, scrapped the curtains and started on the decorations. Finally they polished every bit of natural timber, metal and glass. A set of hat and coat hooks were found to be brass under the black coating. Meanwhile they were collecting a fine assortment of bits and pieces, old prints, small framed mirrors, sepia photographs, even holiday snapshots brought in by their new customers, who were not a few. To these they later added a few horse brasses, hunting crops and the like.

Now, the low ceiling of the Tap Room and the walls above the dado are semi-gloss painted a pale straw colour, and the dado is brush-grained a dark oak shade – though to be frank if it had been up to me I would have chosen something a little paler in this bar. The quarry floor has been treated with linseed oil to give it a lustre. The worst of the tables have been chucked out, and two or three with well-built underframes have been given new hardwood tops. The padded seat has been re-covered in brown, and new wooden stools with turned legs and dished timber tops have been provided. Most of the wall above the dado is covered with pictures, from the local and topical to the esoteric and old-fashioned. Again, I question the appropriateness of all this in a Tap Room, but no-one has complained. The fluorescent tubes have gone, and simple timber wall brackets with amber parchment shades have been fixed and wired. The counter has a new oak top, wax-polished rather than lacquered, which might have looked too sharp and 'new'. Behind it the shelves have been painted black and filled with a magnificent display of wines and spirits above a row of thrawled beer casks, from which a fine variety of 'traditional' beer is served.

The Parlour, from which the servery can also be seen, has received treatment rather similar to that in the Tap, except for the carpet and the use of slightly more expensive looking tables, with chairs and stools upholstered in red leathercloth. The counter front has been painted black and the new top is of mahogany. The curtains are of deep brown with a narrow green stripe. In addition to the array of pictures and bric-à-brac two fairly large framed mirrors have been fixed to the walls opposite the counter and the window respectively. The light shades are of deep Burgundy translucent fabric, and to supplement the new wall fittings a decorative brass table lamp has been placed on the window cill.

Nothing much more really needs to be done. In a pub as small as this there is no need to spend money on structural alterations in order to project a welcome. The licensee can do it himself for each customer, overcoming by personal effort the disadvantage of having to serve through a slot. If the small rooms are sympathetically coloured and furnished the people will automatically feel secluded and can hardly avoid being sociable. When it comes to continuity, all one has to do in a genuine old building is firmly to exclude the more intolerable of the anachronisms inherent in the situation, and in such surroundings there is nothing to prevent the licensee's own brand of goodheartedness from permeating the scene.

A few questions to which we can only guess the answers remain in this case. Why did the brewery not realise the house's potential? Did they look at the place at all, or only at the small barrelage? Did they consider the pub's size? If they did look at these things, why was the minimal outlay required to improve the surfaces, contents and lighting not forthcoming? Did they prefer to build expensive new licensed premises elsewhere rather than ensure intensive trading in existing 'sales area'? Or did they spend oodles of money at a pub down the road where the trade increase could only be commensurately limited? Is there, in fact, a moral to the tale from which breweries in general can learn?

5 The Hibernia

In quite the most cosmopolitan street in a cosmopolitan seaport stands 'The Hibernia', looking slightly lost among the foreign restaurants, sex cinemas and amusement arcades; even the interior seems rather out of keeping with the neighbourhood, as though it had been transplanted from a suburban shopping centre. The single bar occupies the whole of the 12 m frontage and is about the same depth, but half-way down one side the party wall has a 2.5 m step in it so that the rear of the house is that much narrower. The servery juts out forwards and sideways from the projecting angle in a 270° arc, 5.2 m in diameter. There is a little circular office in the middle, and from the far side a further straight length of counter extends some 3 m towards the rear. Snacks are now served from this straight length, but in addition there is a disused snack counter opposite, 6 m long, one end of it tucked under the stairs to the first floor. Not that this waste of space matters very much, because the place is seldom full of people and even if it were the counter over 20 m long would be more than adequate for the 90 m² of drinking area.

The height of the ceiling is 3.5 m, except for an alcove at the rear which is nearly 1 m lower, and above which is a row of clerestorey windows. At each end of the frontage are double entrance doors, and the tall windows between them have horizontal glazing bars. It seems that in the 1930's the whole of the Victorian interior was gutted and refitted with fixtures in the Odeon style, while the external façade was covered with beige faience tiles. The ceiling has a pattern of nine shallow recesses, each about 1 m diameter, from which the light fittings depend. There is a frieze 500 mm deep painted the same deep nicotine shade as the ceiling, and the wallpaper has a small floral pattern giving an overall brownish effect. Piers and other details are picked out in a deep brick red. The dado and counter front are of oak-faced plywood and the top is inlaid with red linoleum. The almost circular display fitting is a better-than-average example of 1930's design, with convex mirrors behind the shelving. It is surmounted by an inverted lighting trough on the face of which translucent lettering announces the brewery name and that of an obsolete brand of beer.

The whole floor is covered with red patterned carpet and the seats with red buttoned moquette. Three U-shaped seating bays occupy the front wall between the two entrance doors, and there are a few other lengths here and there. Tub chairs and stools are upholstered to match the seating, but some are in grave disrepair. The new rectangular cast-iron tables have good polished hardwood tops. A red velvet curtain has been hung above the disused snack counter, but the windows have none and instead a mass of foliage grows up from internal window boxes. There is a large plain mirror in a gilt frame, and a few modern advertising mirrors with crude colouring and ill-made wooden frames. The pendant lights are fitted with large, tall, dome-shaped red translucent fabric shades.

One trouble with the Hibernia is that in an outrageous district it is mundane to the point of boredom. Anywhere else its unassuming nature would be a virtue, but here the demand is either for the abysmally sleazy or for the highly respectable – there is no middle-of-the-road custom so it falls between two bar stools, and similarly the trade is far from spectacular. Many of the local houses do rather more business in less than half the floor area, and so there is clearly room for improvement in such a location, teeming with tourists and 'pleasure'-seekers of all kinds. Our difficulty at the outset is that so little fault can really be found with any specific detail of the place as it is. The amount of open floor space is not very excessive, and the great 270° arc of the counter breaks the room up well. The decorations and furnishings are, on the whole, of good appearance, and the lighting, though unexciting, is reasonable. Obviously something more than a facelift will be needed here.

Enquiry has revealed the fact that the various categories of trade in the area do not mix with each other. Restaurateurs from one Mediterranean country avoid the company of caterers from another. Cinema operators do not mix with theatre staff and British shopkeepers tend to shun the tourists – at any rate while they are off-duty. Each type of local custom uses smallish pubs it has made its own. But the Hibernia is too big to take advantage of that approach. It is one large bar. Surely, then, our first step must be to divide it up into compartments. Ironically enough, that is just what it was like before it was 'modernised'.

New counters are costly, and the one we have is not all that offensive, so we can achieve our aim by leaving it where it is and subdivide the space by means of low radial screens, say 1.8 m high by 1 m wide, placed end on to the counter and glazed in the upper half. There will be three of these, creating two 45° sectors, one at the rear and the other at one side, with two 90° sectors between, each of which will be further divided by a similar screen, somewhat longer, placed at right angles to the front wall of the pub and to the straight party wall respectively. So we have divided the counter into four lengths and the space into four areas which alternate with each other – a truly maze-like arrangement the labyrinthine effect of which will be accentuated by the formation of a false ceiling 2.5 m above floor level, following the arc of the counter but extended to the outer ends of the radial screens over the heads of the standing drinkers. Each group of customers is therefore linked to the serving staff but remains sufficiently secluded from the others. Minor adjustments only will be needed to the front seating bays.

Here we have the layout of a multi-mood compartmented single-bar pub. Each of the three compartments will have its own character but prices will be the same throughout. Reading anti-clockwise from the rear we shall have Bar A, which will be like a Public; Bar B which will resemble a Saloon Bar, at the front near the left-hand entrance; and Bar C which we may call the Lounge occupying the right-hand front. Thus A and B share a 90° arc of counter, while B and C share another.

From the rear (or Public) bar we must remove the old snack counter and replace it with two bays of polished timber seating, with horizontally boarded back and seat shaped to the human form, rather like slatted garden seating but without the drainage gaps. The wall above the seats will be covered completely with mirrors in generous framing. In the niche at the back of the room will be concentrated all the machines, and we may even install a few more of the 'video' type since this is the right sort of neighbourhood for such things: but the volume will be regulated and there will be no loudspeaker in the Lounge. A couple of large green notice boards will fill the remaining vacant wall space in the rear bar.

The new false ceiling over the servery and apron is common to all bars, and we shall choose a ceiling paper with a small all-overish pattern, blackish in effect, and glazed. In the Public and Saloon the existing decorations can be repeated except that the piers and detail will be in deep bottle green, not red. The Public will have a floor of 'Rosewood' lino, and this will be extended into the other bars as an apron 1 m wide, linking the ends of the radial screens all round the foot of the counter. The Saloon and the Lounge will have the best of the existing carpet, relaid: (it is only a few years old). The ceiling must of course be the same in the whole bar area, but the Lounge walls will be covered with a paper as extravagant, multi-coloured and striking in appearance as can be found. From it a suitable colour will be chosen for the frieze in order to link it with the ceiling, and another for the Draylon seating. The Saloon Bar seating, though, will be covered with a shiny black leathercloth, and this will also be used for loose chairs and low stools in both front bars. The tall stools, however, will be saddle-seats with turned legs throughout the pub, and the Public will be furnished with Captain's chairs, along with a few genuine old kitchen chairs and stools, well polished. Tables in all the bars will be the existing ones, painted black and gilt and with the tops renovated. A standing-table will be put in the Public and the Saloon, but not in the Lounge. The large framed mirror will remain on the Lounge wall, and we shall have to get at least two more to cover a fair proportion of the exotic wallpaper. Under the windows the luxuriant greenery will remain, and might well be picked out with pencil-beam spots, possibly green, though the effect from outside would have to be carefully studied.

Ten downlighters deeply recessed into the new false ceiling and placed vertically above the rear edge of the counter top will illuminate the servery, with about five eyeball fittings directed towards the display. Towards the outer edge of the false ceiling will be a ring of downlighters spaced about 120 mm apart. The rest of the space in all three bars will be lit by double amber-shaded wall brackets, and six of the existing pendants will be sited over the seats near the windows. In the Lounge two or three table lamps will be added on the spandrels of the seat capping.

Now it only remains to replace the bits and pieces of non-matching obscure glass in windows and doors with new, possibly (if we can afford it) acid-etched with a shamrock pattern to suit the name of the house, to tidy up the wiring which now trails loose all over the place, and to fit a good heavy tubular brass footrail all round the counter. Fortunately we do not have to look for a new manager – he is one of those genial but strong-minded and strong-armed Irishmen the loss of whom (together with their charming and highly intelligent wives) would drastically impoverish the English pub scene.

Part IV

DESIGN GUIDE
by Frank Bradbeer

1 Design Check-List

The architect working on design of a pub will all too often have less than complete control of all design stages. The client, usually a brewery, may supply a very detailed brief and may treat the fitting-out and furnishing of the building as a completely separate exercise. However, there are six basic stages in construction or alteration of a pub. This is not to say that the stages are always rigidly adhered to, nor that it is necessary to do so. But if those stages are recognised, the designer will be thinking clearly about the subject, and can make up his own mind what to do. The first and last stages may not even involve the architect at all; they must be mentioned to complete the picture.

The architect may be called in at virtually any stage. He may be commissioned to provide sketches at an early stage of the process, or he may be called in at the end to furnish and fit someone else's scheme.

If an architect is called in at a later stage, unless he has a wide experience of designing pubs, he should trace the progress through stages 1 and 2 Feasibility, plus stages 3 and 4 if he is involved at stage 5. To be involved at a late stage does not excuse lack of knowledge of the early stages although, naturally, the spade work will not have to be done again. The stages involved are:

1 Commercial feasibility
The client, normally a brewer, makes a study and decides that a licensed house (or extension or alteration of a licensed house) in a certain area is a commercial proposition.

2 Inception and primary brief
The client crystallises a basic scheme sufficient for an architectural feasibility study to be done. In practice, the scope of this stage can vary enormously, for it can lead (although it should not) to a fairly firm outline proposal, accepted in some cases by the client (often a board of directors). Ideally it should lead to a sketch design on which to base a decision to go ahead, and complete the other stages.

3 Secondary brief
The aim here is to establish all remaining details, so that an outline proposal may be submitted and formally approved. Although in this guide primary and secondary briefs are mentioned, the secondary brief stage may take the form of meetings or telephone conversations which gradually establish the form of the outline proposals. The more thorough this stage is, the more efficient will be the final stages. It is in fact the stage of exhaustive research into the aspect of public house design which is most closely concerned with the peculiarities of the trade.

4 Outline proposals

All the details from the two previous briefs will be collated to form a scheme for approval by the client. The scheme is usually drafted to 1:100 scale, so that the drawings submitted to the client will also be the basis of the drawings submitted to the licensing authority, thus saving unnecessary work in the drawing office.

At this stage the scheme is frozen and the licensing application will be made.

These drawings will also be the basis of the application for Planning consent and clearly, any departure now from the extablished scheme will involve the risk of long delays.

5 Scheme design

The basic 1:100 scale drawings submitted at stage 4 will now be transformed into working drawings. It is important to adhere rigidly to the outline proposal drawings used for application to licensing magistrates, since any significant alteration to the drawings will entail another application. Ideally, this stage should be considered in conjunction with, indeed as part of, stage 6 Detail design. In practice, stage 6 may be the responsibility of a specialist while an outside architect may receive his commission at stage 5. This is to be deplored, since clearly the two stages should at worst be considered together and at best be more than the seed of an idea at secondary brief stage.

If it is known that a specialist is handling stage 6, and contact is established while working drawings are in hand, there is the possibility of a more satisfactory final result, although the task is easier for the architect handling stage 5 if he completes his 'carcass' drawings and hands them over to the specialist to carry on from there. In the case of specialists acting for commercial firms there is much to be said for this, whereas in the case of freelance designers specialising in interiors, a relationship is often easy to establish at stage 5 or even stage 4.

These drawings will be the basis of the application for approval under the Building Regulations by the Fire Officer. As with other building types, time will probably be saved if a dialogue can be started with Building Inspector and the Fire Officer before these drawings are completed.

It is characteristic of many pub rooms that some of the most suitable materials carry a fire hazard, eg timber. The extent of these finishes should be established in principle at this stage and the necessary agreements reached. In the case of an existing house, great care must be taken at this stage because a small alteration or improvement may open the flood gates to demands by the Fire Officer. Large sheets of glass in fire doors are anathema to Fire Officers, no matter how beautifully they are brilliant-cut of acid-etched. Very likely they will be found to open the wrong way. Changes of level, stairs and balustrades may all come under scrutiny and one may lose much of the favourable character by having to concede what in all conscience can sometimes be the irrational demands of an official who is paid to administer the very letter of the law. Building Regulations when applied to existing buildings are notoriously and sometimes ludicrously inept and architects involved in the restoration alteration and refurbishing of pubs are directly in the line of fire.

6 Detail design

In the event the actual scope of this stage may vary. It might consist of all the bar fittings, fixed seating, soft furnishings, electrics, furniture and so on constituting a complete scheme of interior decoration. On the other hand, it may consist of 'bar fittings' only, including perhaps the bar counter, back bar fitting and perhaps the fixed seats. Clearly, if the same architects who have handled the project from the beginning undertake this stage, its scope can be increased to the point where it is happily intergrated with the structure inside the house and out. On the other hand, it is a convenient stage for the work to be handed over to a specialist, and in this case it is important to establish exactly where responsibilities lie: a more difficult task than merely establishing a cost limit, since it will vary with the brewer. Even within one brewery tenancy agreements may not always be the same, so that a tenant in one house may have more power to influence a scheme than a tenant in another. A manager will probably have very little influence at all.

The designer of stage 6 may find that some of the money which he is spending may have been put up by the tenant and a great deal of tact and care may be required because of this.

Having gone this far, it must be made very clear that these stages are to some extent academic, and may very easily overlap. However, if it can be appreciated that these stages exist, if only in the mind, a check can be kept on the sort of position which should be achieved at any given point, and, more especially, the kind of mental attitude that should be adopted towards the work.

The clerk to the licensing magistrates is an important figure, and a firm which approaches the design of licensed houses for the first time will find his knowledge of local conditions and the preferences of the local justices valuable. However, it must be remembered that while his advice may be helpful, some magistrates' clerks develop notions of exaggerated authority and this might prove a difficulty. The clerk will also have some idea of what the police requirements normally are; the blessing of both the police and the fire officer is required before working drawings are undertaken at stage 5 Scheme design.

A complication in public house design is the varied nature of the client's own organisation. An architect once commissioned does not want to take instructions from more than one source, even though clients' decisions are often made by different people at different times. Paragraph 4 of the design guide covers this, and rigid adherence to agreements on questions of authority and discretion will avoid unnecessary trouble, even if at times the procedure seems tedious.

In paragraph 5 the scope of the brief is established. An architect appointed at stage 6 must refer back to this paragraph, since the final stage may be complicated by tenancy agreements,

brewery policy, or prior agreements with an architect who has been commissioned to be responsible for the project up to stage 6. For instance, who is to be responsible for lighting fittings, loose furniture, clocks, soft furnishings bells, beer dispensing equipment, piped music and so on? If these do not figure as a lump sum in the contract price, probably as a provision in the bills of quantity, it is very important to establish what figure is allowed and how it is to be administered.

The tendency with public houses, as with most other building types, is to include as much as possible as measured items in the bills of quantity. The obvious advantage here (apart from purely contractural advantages) is that, if this is to be done, there is a much better chance that the scheme will be considered in all its aspects at an early stage, so that one architect will be responsible for as much of the scheme as possible. For specialists to be employed to do the bar fitting and interior decoration is as unsatisfactory as it is discouraging for the architect who has really designed a scheme as an entity from the outset, only to see it undergo metamorphosis in its last stage.

1 Inception and primary brief

This corresponds with stage A of the RIBA 'Plan of work', and its object as already defined, is to establish sufficient information about the project to enable feasibility to be assessed and to set the broad framework within which the later stages are to be evolved. In the case of a public house it is probable that the client has established commercial feasibility before approaching an architect.

1 Type of licence
Ascertain type of licence desired by client. Licensing procedures will affect whole design and building programme.

2 Type of client

The client may be in one of the following categories.

Brewing company

This will have a number of tied houses, run by either tenants or managers. Managers are unlikely to have much connection with the architect, but tenants will have some financial interest in fittings and furnishings and may become involved in stage 5.

Operating company

The relationship with the parent brewer will be defined in the lease and legal agreements, but the properties themselves will almost certainly be controlled by a manager, who will have no official contact with the architect. Groups of free houses are also run in this way.

Individual who owns and runs a free house

The owner/manager will be closely interested at all stages.

Ownership

Determine ownership. Most brewers own the freeholds but in the case of a leasehold examine conditions of lease. Terms of lease may preclude some of client's intentions.

Client's organisation

Establish knowledge of the client's organisation. Architects, surveyors and estates departments of brewing companies may all be involved in addition to the legal department, accountants and the head brewer who may have wide powers.

Legal advice

Legal matters are normally handled by a brewer's own legal department, or a solicitor commissioned for this purpose. In the case of an individual free house a solicitor should be specially appointed, who has experience of licensing application.

3 Site details

It is unlikely that a project will be considered beyond the commercial feasibility stage unless a site is available or has been acquired.

Location

Establish exact location of site, also preliminary site details and limitations.

Availability

Establish when site will become available.

4 Space requirements

Determine in broad outline the accommodation and facilities required.

Size of various licensed rooms:
- public bar
- tap room
- saloon bar
- smoke room
- bar parlour
- lounge
- cocktail bar
- American bar
- music rooms requiring a special license
- rooms for private meetings

Determine sizes of the various licensed rooms. This may have been done by the client at the commercial feasibility stage, and will depend on an assessment of the local population and its drinking habits.

Ratio of servery to licensed area

The client will probably have views on what the ratio of servery area to licensed area should be, based on previous experience. This may be expressed as 1 m run of bar counter to so many m^2 of licensed area in front of the counter.

Ratio of storage to licensed area:

Determine amount of storage area the client regards as adequate for the project. This is a function of the estimated capacity of the house in terms of converted barrels expressed in number of barrels per week.

Storage methods

Determine storage methods, ie, bulk, keg, cases, etc.

Delivery methods

Determine frequency and types of vehicle involved. Police may insist that drays leave the highway to unload.

Off-sales department

Determine storage and service space required.

Staff spaces

Separate staff space not normally a requirement.

Licensee's living accommodation

Determine overall area of licensee's accommodation. The local licensing justices will insist that accommodation is adequate. 100m^2 plus garage is normally acceptable.

Catering

Determine whether catering is envisaged and if so the scope.

Other spaces

Determine whether client has any requirements for space arising from some special circumstances or from any special way of working, eg skittle alley, meeting rooms.

External spaces:

Car park

The client may have views on car parking facilities and the minimum laid down by the local planning authority may not be the governing factor.

The car park should be planned to interfere as little as possible with general amenities, but the customer should be able to see the access route clearly and preferably the car park itself, as this seems to have a psychological effect: a split sec-

ond decision to stop and park may be the result of seeing a half-empty car park. Establish that access will have the approval of the local authority. More parking space may be needed in future and this may affect siting of park.

Drinking areas

Bowling, putting, children's play areas, gardens. Many public houses have land attached which is capable of being made available to customers who wish to sit outside. With skilled planning such land can materially increase sales and summer evenings can become extremely profitable.

5 Costs

Cost limitations

Establish cost limitations, and ascertain whether there is to be any division or breakdown of the total cost, either within different departments of a brewery, between the brewery and the tenant, or for commercial reasons.

6 Programme

The programme will almost certainly be geared to the sessions of the licensing justices and financial year of brewing company. It is more than likely that the detailed programme will not be established until stage 3 (secondary brief). But when transfer of licences is concerned programmed dates must be met.

7 Administration

Contract policy

Establish form of contract to be used.

Liaison procedures

Establish who will be in charge of overall liaison between client bodies and architect, and degree of his responsibility.

Form of client's approval

Establish the form which the client's approval of the design team's decisions should take.

Client's advisers

Determine function and responsibilities and whether direct approach by the architect is possible or permissible

Appointment of architect and consultants

As noted, the architect may be appointed at any one of a number of stages. Establish at time of appointment the extent of the service to be provided and the basis for fees; this may include quantity surveyor, mechanical services consultants, structural engineer, etc.

2 Feasibility

This stage corresponds with stage B of the RIBA 'Plan of work', and the data obtained in stage 1 (primary brief) are here studied and analysed to reach a decision on the feasibility of the project. It is very likely that feasibility will have been established, possibly in an extremely sketchy way, by a brewer's own estates or architects department. The architect should use this stage as a check list, and in any case certain steps, such as site investigation, should be carried out at this stage.

8 Site studies

Site investigation is especially important if a basement cellar is required.

Planning permission

It must be established that a public house will be permitted on the site or that extensions of alterations will be accepted.

Access and deliveries

Conditions may be imposed by the local authority with regard to access both for the public, whether to the car park or perhaps direct from street to licensed rooms, and for delivery vehicles and general arrangements for delivery.

Circulation of vehicles

It is desirable at this stage to know the probable car park area, access and exit routes and delivery proposals.

Surrounding or existing buildings

Assess rights of light, existing easements and so on, and the effect of adjacent buildings generally.

Levels

Will affect decision as to type of cellar and general layout of house.

Views

May affect layout of rooms.

Building of historic interest

When altering or rebuilding an existing public house, ascertain by inquiry of local authority whether preservation orders apply to either the whole building or to any of the features.

9 Basic design

At this stage it should be possible to work out approximate form of building.

Form of building

Licensed rooms
Must be arranged to permit economical service and supervision.

Servery areas
Must be compact, easy to work and linked to storage areas.

Storage areas
Should be at ground level or below, with easy delivery access. May need environmental control and space for plant. Cellars at first floor are possible.

Circulation
Should not take up much space. Much circulation will be to and from lavatories which must be positioned carefully.

Licensee's accommodation
Normally at upper level but kitchen/dining-room may be on ground floor.

10 Costs

Prepare outline cost studies

Special breakdowns of costs may be required to satisfy various departments of client's firm, eg bar fitting and furnishings may be dealt with separately from basic structure.

11 Legislation

Apart from compliance with building regulations and planning controls, public house buildings must satisfy requirements of the licensing magistrates and local police. It is impossible to forecast these requirements so the architect should have early discussions with the clerk to the justices, police chief and fire officer.

12 Feasibility report and proposals

Prepare report on feasibility and submit to client.

3 Secondary brief

This stage is part of stage C of the RIBA 'Plan of work'. Since it is the stage at which an architect in private practice is very likely to be called in, it is necessary to establish a great deal of the detail of general background to the project in particular and public house design in general.

The actual position achieved may vary from one project to another. Some brewers work out a complete scheme at the end of stage 2 which may have been accepted in principle by the board. On the other hand, the architect called in at this stage may be confronted with a bare site on which the brewers have done minimal research to convince themselves that the project is feasible *subject to a magistrate's licence*. In any event, an architect first involved at this stage will make it his business to go through the previous stages outlined in this guide.

13 Circulation

The circulation pattern will be critical and client's views should be obtained.

Segregation of trade

To provide completely separate systems for different classes of trade will be expensive (ie public bar, lounge cocktail bar etc.)

Lavatories

In a two-roomed pub, one set of lavatories for each sex can serve both rooms.

In a three- (or more) roomed house it may be that one set of lavatories will be planned to serve the two more expensive rooms, and one set serve perhaps public bar only.

Interested parties

Local justices, police and fire officer will all be interested in the public spaces and related circulation; the architect should have preliminary discussions with the clerk to the justices, police and fire officer. Their basic interest will be supervision and maintenance of an orderly house, means of escape and means of ejection. Police may want a door with space outside for a van to permit unobtrusive arrest. If they are not satisfied as to any aspect, they may recommend the licensing magistrates not to consent to the scheme.

14 Storage

Check that all information affecting quantity and mode of storage has been collected. Cooling may be in the cellar or in the servery area.

15 Outstanding items

Check that all items in the primary brief have been covered; this being especially important if the architect did not receive the primary brief.

Equipment

List all special equipment that may have to be accommodated.

Cooling plant
Cellar and servery

Hoists and conveyor
Associated cellar flaps, rolling ways. Auto hoists may be manual or electric.

Beer raising equipment
For an illustration of the standard electric cellar pump see fig **12** on p. 142.

Enclosing elements and finishes
Determine brewery policy and whether this is to be rigidly applied

16 Appointment of architect and special consultants
If the architect is first involved at this stage, it will be necessary to establish the extent of the service. Specialist bar fitters, interior designers, engineers and electricians may be appointed by the client.

17 Programme
The programme must now be finally established, and agreed with all interested parties.

4 Outline proposals

This stage is the remainder of stage c of the RIBA 'Plan of work' and determines the general approach to layout, design and construction to the point where one definite scheme is produced and agreed by the consultants, and put forward as a recommended solution to the client.

18 Preliminaries
Investigate all client nominees (subcontractors and suppliers) as to availability, cost and suitability. Brewers tend to be more rigid in their attitudes to nominated subcontractors than many clients, since they tend to use the same subcontractors for many different contracts, and in the field of bar fitting the choice is naturally limited. Visit similar projects.

Insurances
Advice may be sought from the client's legal department.

19 Detailed site information
Carry out detailed site investigation and other relevant inquiries.

20 Outline planning studies
In accordance with para 9, planning studies can be made to determine the best general layout. See p. 140.

Space requirements
Check space requirements to ensure that there has been no change since commercial feasibility stage, either in public licensed areas or in staff and storage areas (perhaps occasioned by changed storage methods or delivery schedules).

Relationship of storage to servery
Assuming a good relationship of delivery access to storage, the next stage is to ensure smooth and direct passage from storage to servery, whether for draught or bottled beer, or other beverages coming bottled and normally packed in cases.

Decide whether beer is to be stored at ground floor level, above or below, the latter involving the use of a rolling way and case hoist. High level storage should be avoided if possible.

Ensure that heating plant will not affect temperature of cellar and that heating ducts do not interfere with beer ducts to dispensing points.

Relationship of servery to public rooms
The servery area is ideally a single space connecting all the licensed rooms and permitting staff to pass freely from one licensed room to another, making for economic deployment of staff, easy supervision, and simplifying stocking up, cleaning and general working of the servery areas.

Supervision
Adequate supervision from the servery over all licensed areas will be required by the justices.

Security
It must not be possible for customers to pilfer over the end of the bar, or gain unobserved access.

Counter

The bar counter itself is perhaps the most important item of furniture and will be a major factor in inducing the right sort of atmosphere in the room. Its character may change according to the type of room involved.

Planning of individual rooms

The licensed rooms, to be successful, must be comfortable, both physically and psychologically. Many believe that psychological comfort combined with a degree of physical discomfort increase sales of beer.

Planning of special areas

If special uses are envisaged, such as singing, dancing and games, these should be planned to become part of the general environment, unless a room is given over entirely to the activity concerned. (In this case, eg a music room, the whole atmosphere of the room will be dictated by the special activity.) Whether standing at the bar or sitting at tables customers must be able to see the performance. Darts, bar billiards, shove ha'penny, and so on, should neither disrupt the general conduct of the room nor be tucked away as a thing apart, but should be incorporated as a general background to the life of the room.

Relationship of customers' lavatories to public licensed areas

Having ascertained whether customers are to be segregated or not, lavatories should be planned for easy access from the bars, and so that casual use by non-customers is discouraged. The lavatories should be simply planned, with no nooks or crannies, so that they are easily cleaned and do not allow accidental misuse, to say nothing of more deliberate misdemeanour. Entrances to men's and women's lavatories should not be too close together.

Off-licence shop

If an off-licence shop is to be included, staff access ought to be from the main servery area, but there should be no public communication between the shop and other public areas. This enables a separate licence to be granted out of normal licensing hours if required.

21 Environment

Natural lighting

High daylight levels are not usually necessary.

Artificial lighting

Important factor in pub atmosphere.

Licensed areas

1 High level of overall lighting of even intensity is to be avoided.
2 Fluorescent tubes are generally unsatisfactory.
3 Indirect light sources, such as cornice lighting, are generally unsatisfactory.
4 Multiple points of tungsten light are usually more conducive to a good atmosphere.

Servery

Light in the servery needs to be at a higher level than that in the public area but unpleasant contrast must be avoided. Display lighting in the servery can take the form of spotlights concealed behind the fascia above the bar, or of strips in the backfitting.

Circulation areas and customers' lavatories

Should be adequate but economic and robust

Storage

Intermittent use. A reasonably high level should be provided for practical and hygenic reasons. Fluorescents permissable.

Forecourt lighting

Avoid low level floods which can distract drivers using car park or adjacent roads.

External advertising

An integral part of pub design. Planning consents necessary.

Private quarters

Normal domestic standards

134

May be required if licence is for music, singing and dancing.

Heating and ventilation

Temperature in range 65°–70°f (18°–21°c). Heating and cooling equipment must be responsive to rapid changes in temperature.

Acoustics

Noise from one room should not be allowed to dominate other rooms.

Music rooms may need to be insulated from rest of house. Juke box or background music the norm.

22 Services

Water

Drinking water is required in services at various points in addition to normal cold water supply. Hot water to sinks, glass washers, etc.

Electricity

Need for supply point for special equipment in addition to normal heating and lighting.

Gas

Possible gas fired heating mock open fires etc.

Refrigeration

In cellar; on pipeline; cold shelves.

Music

Relayed music and Juke box

Avoid mounting speakers where they will disturb customers, eg on low fascias over the bar.

Telephone

Intercom.

Plant spaces and ducts

Decide location, size of location of plant spaces. Note that refrigerated shelves require their own plant located nearby or incorporated into shelves. "On line" cooling often located under bar.

Special services

Hoists are commonly hand operated. Bottle disposer. Beer dispensing equipment. Electric hoists disproportionately expensive.

23 Structure

The structure is likely to be of a domestic nature, but owing to its larger size and more complicated plan form, greater structural spans may be involved, and heavy dead loads due to fire proof construction.

Fire insulation

Public houses are normally two-storey structures, the upper floor being tenant's accommodation, with perhaps a few guest bedrooms. Fire resisting construction is therefore necessary between the two floors. See above.

Effect of ancillary volumes

Since in a public house the upper floor is normally devoted to tenant's accomodation, the tendency is for there to be large ground floor volume, with a disproportionately small upper floor volume, with the consequent need to support large areas of external wall at first floor level over ground floor voids. This suggests the use of columns, often in licensed areas, which can be used with advantage in creating interesting spaces, and are in fact, part of the traditional idiom.

Special loads

Provide for special loads such as dancing, beer storage and plant areas.

24 Security

Where valuable stocks of spirits and tobacco are held, special steps may need to be taken to prevent pilfering, and this may mean a separate secure store for more valuable stocks. This will usually be within the main bottle store.

25 Maintenance

Consider maintenance and cleaning, both external and internal, in relation to capital cost.

Public houses are subject to heavy wear and tear, therefore durable finishes are necessary.

26 Present scheme and report to the client
The scheme put forward to the client will be the basis of the application to the licensing justices. Once the client has accepted it, no further alterations should be made and the way is clear to make formal application to the justices. Any subsequent alteration to the licensed areas will entail a further application to the justices.

5 Scheme design

This stage corresponds to stage D of the RIBA 'Plan of work', and is concerned with preparing a fully worked out design based on the outline proposals. To save repetition in this stage, and in the next stage, 6 'Detail design', constant reference must be made to the previous stages in the guide. Ideally, this and the next stage should be worked together, but in practice the detail design stage is often separated and a specialist designer is frequently commissioned for it.

6 Detail design

In the case of public houses it is at this stage that interior decoration, including bar fitting, fixed seating, furnishings and so on, is usually designed, approved and detailed, often forming the basis for a separate commission. As in stage 5, constant reference must be made to stage 4 'Outline proposals' for check list and references.

27 Check scope of brief
If this stage is the subject of a separate commission, the designer must establish the scope of his brief.

Bar counter and back bar fitting ie servery area
This includes sinks, cold shelves, dispense points, glass washers, on line coolers, etc.

Fire place
Solid fuel may be considered.

Fixed seating
Different treatments for various rooms.

Floor, wall and ceiling finishes
Should 'weather' with age.

Lighting fittings
General lighting in licensed area.
General lighting in servery area.
Display lighting in servery area.
Special lighting for games and so on.
Emergency lighting for function's rooms.

Beer dispensing equipment
Not normally part of the designer's brief.

Bar sundries
Baskets for empty bottles, bottle openers and dispensers, glass washers, till, and so on. The list here cannot be comprehensive, but if bar sundries form part of the designer's brief, the client should be asked to furnish a complete list of requirements.

Soft furnishings
Carpet, curtains, etc.

Loose furniture
Bar stools, tables, chairs.

Special fittings
Screens, hat and cloak racks.

Clocks
Electric or mechanical.

Special features
Bandstand, stage.

Games
Darts, bar billiards (traditional), dominoes and shove-ha'penny. Pool has now overtaken the popularity of bar billiards (see p. 146). There are no electrical requirements for these except lighting, but some managements may insist on the installation of 'fruit machines' and electronic

games of all kinds. These vary considerably as to size. Vernacular games, ie those local to vicinity.

Relayed music
Loudspeaker grilles for public address and music.

Juke box
Vary very much as to size.

Television
Not advised.

Heating and ventilating
The designer may want to vet fittings, grilles and so on. Heating may be incorporated with seating, ventilation with bar canopy.

Advertising matter
The designer may have some control over 'decorative' advertising, which may be acid etched or brilliant cut glass work in mirrors and windows or in screens, lettering above the counter or in the back fitting, special displays.

Signs
Co-ordinated policy for all signs is essential. Client may have house style.

Mandatory
Licensee's name and scope of licence must be displayed at door and 'exit' signs for functions rooms.

Guidance
Justices will require adequate direction signs for lavatories.

Pictures, bric-à-brac
A sum may be included for this.

Ironmongery
The designer may wish to control ironmongery to windows, doors, special ironmongery for escape doors to functions rooms.

28 Costs
Establish cost limits for stage 6 and source of finance – eg brewer or tenant.

29 Drawings and general information
If this stage is being handled by a specialist, sufficient drawings and a specifiation of the overall scheme must be made available to him so that he can complete his own drawings for estimates to be obtained. The architect must also supply sufficient drawings to satisfy any subcontractor who may be appointed – possibly belonging to the same firm as the specialist consultant.

If the carcass has been agreed, an exchange of basic details between architect and specialist consultant will result in a scheme satisfactory to both. The specialist may not, however, be answerable to the architect responsible for the initial stages; if this is so, the specialist should ascertain who in the client's hierarchy has authority to issue his instructions and confirm his decisions.

Programme
Establish when completion is envisaged; this may be determined by the justices' consent.

Glossary

30 Public house terms

Acid-etched glass Decorative glass with the pattern etched on the reverse side with acid. See also embossed glass
Anaglypta Victorian trade name of a hard-wearing, heavily embossed patterned paper used to line wall and ceiling surfaces and often covered with oil paint
Bar The counter at which the drinks are sold, or a licensed room containing a counter. A licensed room not containing a counter is usually referred to by another name
Back bar fitting (back fitting, sideboard fitting, and so on) The fitting at the back of the

servery behind the bar counter. It accommodates bottled beer, wines, spirits, glasses and bar sundries, and possibly contains refrigerated shelving. It should be regarded as a display and advertising feature. In a modern house, it normally has its own integral lighting and is seen at its best carrying a lively display of bottles and glasses, relieved perhaps by bric-à-brac

Bar sundries Items of bar equipment which do not come under fittings and furnishings, eg till, crown cap openers, cocktail shakers, etc

Bar walk (apron) An area of floor along the front of the bar subject to hard wear and tear and often finished in linoleum or other hard material in lieu of carpet

Beer pull The handle of a manually operated beer pump. A visible sign of what is popularly called 'real ale'

Brewster sessions Annual sessions of the licensing justices, at which licences to trade in alcoholic liquors are issued

Brilliant-cut glass Decorative glass containing stars etc, which are achieved by cutting on a wheel and polishing

Britannia table A three-legged cast-iron table with a circular top, usually with a decorative medallion on each leg which often, but not always, is a representation of Britannia. The head of Queen Victoria, rams' heads, Viking heads or even sporting personalities such as the late W. G. Grace were also used on the medallions. These tables were common in the late 19th century and were an ideal piece of bar furniture, being economic of space, decorative and so heavy that they were difficult to knock over or throw. They are now once again available on the market new

Beer engine A manually-operated pump or range of pumps supplied as an entity to fit into the bar counter. In early days these engines were sometimes installed against a wall

Brush-graining A traditional method of painting timber to imitate wood grain

Cold shelves Refrigerated shelving usually incorporated in the back fitting below the level of the bartop

Confirmation of plans This is given at a meeting of the licensing magistrates after a favourable recommendation by the viewing committee

Converted barrelage A formula by which all liquor sales are converted into the equivalent value of barrels of beer in order to assess the commercial status of the house

Draught beer Generic term for beer in bulk, whether carbonated or natural

Drinking area Licensed area, excluding servery and bar counter, but including fixed seating

Dispense points Points in the servery area, normally on the bar counter, from which beer or other drink is dispensed via a tap by pumps (manual or electric) or by gas pressure

Enamelled glass Also known as 'flashed glass' this consists of clear glass coloured by means of a thin veneer of glass blown on one side only

Free house A public house not owned (or tied) to a brewery. May be owned by the landlord or may be part of a chain owned by a private company who install managers. The freehold may be owned by an institution or large estate who lease to a tenant

Fixed seating Built-in seating in the licensed areas, normally coming under the heading of 'fittings'.

Inbuilt pub House forming part of a larger building such as an office block

Keg beer Generic term for a beer delivered in bulk (normally steel canisters) and dispensed under gas pressure

Licensee The person in whose name the licence is held, possibly a tenant or a manager but not necessarily either

Licensee's accommodation Dwelling accommodation attached to the house (not necessarily inhabited by the licensee, and non-existent in a 'lock-up' pub)

Licence strip Strip above the entrance bearing the licensee's name and the extent of the licence

Licensed area The area accessible to the

public for drinking purposes

Managed house   House run by a manager

Pot shelf   A special shelf, often fixed above or on the bar counter forming a useful element in the internal decor

Optic   An automatic measure fitted to bottles for dispensing spirits etc

Private bar   A small compartment adjacent to and partitioned off from the main bar counter

Rolling way   Steep incline down which barrels run from the cellar flaps

Servery   Area where drinks are dispensed. It is related to the drinking areas and economically becomes a single area running through each licensed room

Snob screens   Decorative pivoting screens, usually of decorated glass, giving a degree of privacy between one drinking space and another

Spirit urn   A decorative china urn usually installed on the bar counter and fitted with a tap for dispensing spirits. These attractive by-gones are now used for decorative purposes only, having been supplanted by the 'optic'. See optic

Settle   A fixed seat, usually thought of as timber

Settle end   The shaped end to a fixed seat

Snug   A small compartment or room not necessarily adjacent to the main bar

Stillion, stilling   Support for a cask or barrel. (The Oxford Dictionary distinguishes between this and 'stillage', a bench or frame for keeping articles off the floor)

Soft furnishings   Items such as carpet and curtains in the licensed area, often paid for by a tenant

Tap-room   The common drinking room of a public house from which the public bar has since evolved

Tied house   Usually owned by a brewery company, but sometimes leased by an institution or private individual to a brewery company. A house tied by trading agreement with a particular brewer

Transfer sessions   Sessions of the licensing justices at intervals during the year between brewster sessions

Wicket   A door, often incorporated in the end of the bar counter, which, with a flap, gives access to the drinking area from the servery

2 Layout And Dimensions

This section sets out the way in which spaces in a public house should be related to each other.

Basic layout

The servery or service area is the hub of the plan and forms a link between public and storage areas.

The servery should be linked with bars, private entrance, off-sales, cellar and yard. A staff lavatory should be accessible from the servery.

There are recent examples of split serveries, but it is normally considered to be essential for the servery to be continuous, interconnecting with the bars and off-licence counter for ease of staffing; particularly during off-peak hours when the pub may be run single-handed for a short period.

The boundary with public areas is the counter and a useful rule of thumb for preliminary planning is 300 mm run of counter for every 2.5 m^2 of drinking area.

Drinking areas

In a two-bar pub these would normally be public and saloon bar or smoke room, but see page 71 on distinctions between bars.

The areas and types of bars will be the outcome of the brewery's commercial feasibility study, in which the potential demand would be assessed in terms of converted barrels.

If the architect is briefed to advise on the architectural feasibility at such a preliminary stage, a useful rule of thumb would be 7.5 m^2 of drinking area per weekly converted barrel in a city, and 10 m^2 in the country.

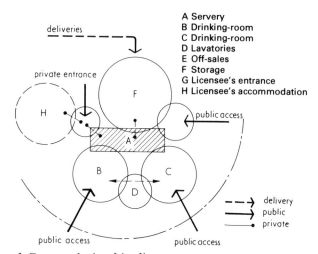

A Servery
B Drinking-room
C Drinking-room
D Lavatories
E Off-sales
F Storage
G Licensee's entrance
H Licensee's accommodation

1 *Space relationship diagram*

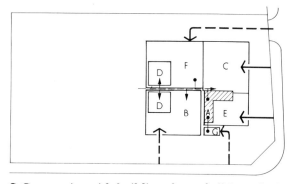

2 *Corner site with building clear of all boundaries*

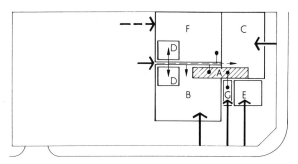

3 *Corner site with building set against back boundary*

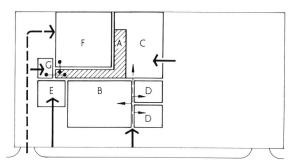

4 *Straight site with delivery access at side*

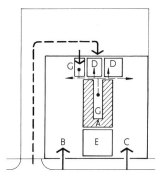

5 *Straight site with delivery access at rear and storage at lower level*

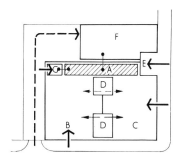

6 *Restricted corner site*

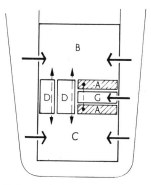

7 *Island site with storage at lower level*

These matters are however strictly under the general policy of the brewery and the architect would normally be provided with such details.

Lavatories

A two-bar pub would normally have one suite of public lavatories serving both bars.

The number of sanitary appliances would be related to the drinking areas served. The licensing justices would need to be satisfied that the facilities were adequate, but an average sized pub totalling 100 m² of drinking area would normally need one wc, five urinal spaces and one lavatory basin for men, and two or three wcs and two basins for women.

The need for one suite of lavatories to serve two bars will impose limits on the variety of planning solutions possible.

Off-sales

This must be accessible from the servery but must not give the public access to drinking areas. It will need a separate entrance.

Storage

The main storage area will usually be a cellar at a lower level than the servery.

For preliminary planning the storage area should be at least two-thirds the size of the total drinking area.

Licensee's accommodation

A private entrance should be provided for the licensee, to give access to living accommodation and servery.

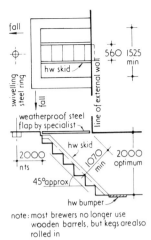

8 *Cellar flap and barrel chute for use with storage below ground*
Note: Most brewers no longer use wooden barrels, but kegs are also rolled in

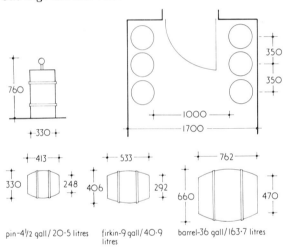

9 *Cellarage for barrels and kegs:*
a *Keg with valve attachment*
b *Metal barrels*
c *Bar store with kegs*

pin-4½ gall/20·5 litres   firkin-9 gall/40·9 litres   barrel-36 gall/163·7 litres

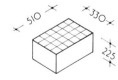

10 *Case storage. Each case contains 24 half-pint bottles. Non-standard cases are normally smaller*
a *Typical case*
b *Plan of case cellarage*
c *Alternative plan*

Dimensions

Often, particularly in older properties, the charm or customer appeal can lie in the eccentricity, or even the inconvenience, of the layout. The planning of public areas depends on the flair and experience of the designer. Optimum seating may not be possible (or even desirable) and the clever designer will turn this to advan-

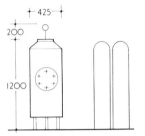

11 *Bulk storage with typical CO_2 canisters. Larger canisters exist*

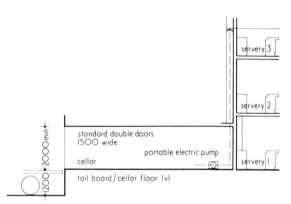

12 *Beer supplied through several storeys from ground level cellar. Standard electric cellar pump will raise beer up to 9 metres*

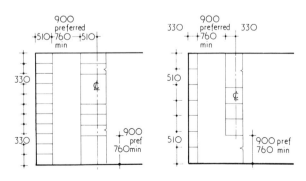

tage. However, in the areas where the staff do their work, and where the liquor is stored, specific dimensional requirements assume great importance and closely affect the efficient running of the establishment.

Requirements peculiar to the pub are:
- drink delivery
- drink storage
- drink dispensing

Drink delivery
Vehicles deliver drink in bulk (by tanker), in barrel (or keg), or by bottle.

Drink storage
The vehicular access must be convenient for the cellars, which may be below ground, **8** at ground level, or in rare cases at an upper level.

The cellar must be planned to store the following in an economic manner:
- barrels, or, more likely, kegs, **9**
- bottles, usually in cases stacked on top of one another, **10**
- wine and spirits, usually stacked in a separate store on shelves
- bulk storage tanks, **11**

The wooden barrel accommodated on a tilting stillage is now extremely rare. The size of a case containing two dozen half-pint bottles is fairly standard, **10a**, as is the standard metal keg, **9**. These are the common modules of beer storage.

Storage of empties is based on the same standards, except that it is easy to stack empty cases higher and therefore less area is required.

Any beer other than in bottles or cans is (for the purposes of design) referred to as 'draught'. Draught beer from below ground, or ground level cellarage is usually delivered under pressure. Beer travelling upwards one storey height is usually pumped electrically, **12**.

Bottled beer travelling upwards one storey height is usually delivered by a case hoist, **13**, which is installed as a unit and can be manually or electrically operated. Manual operation is simpler and considerably cheaper.

Drink dispensing
There are three elements to the servery, **14**:
- the bar counter
- the back bar fitting
- the servery space between

The length of the counter, **15**, will depend on circumstance, but the height and width can be regarded as standard within narrow limits. The width can be reduced in special circumstances,

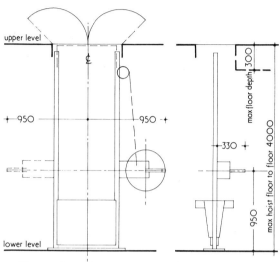

a *Front elevation*   **b** *Side elevation*

13 *Small manual case hoist for two cases:*
c *Plan at upper level*

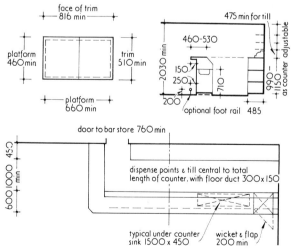

14 *Typical bar servery:*
a *Plan*
b *Section*

but the need to accommodate at least one sink will be an important factor. Glasses may be stored in racks above the counter, and standard heights are important, **16**. The servery space may be regarded as a standard width in most cases. This is governed by the ease of working as opposed to economy of area.

The back bar fitting will comprise a sideboard top, often at the same height as the bar counter. Below this level will be stored bottled beer, sometimes on cooled shelves. These are fairly standard items, **17**, **18**.

Above the sideboard top will be a display fitting which may accommodate spirits (often with 'optics'), glasses and other products (including wine). Adjustable shelves are useful. The lowest shelf must be high enough to accommodate loose bottles, siphons, the till etc.

The sizes of special equipment such as coolers, glass washers etc should be determined from consultation with the client as to preferred manufacturers. The sizes of ducts for the beer pipes, which are usually lagged, should be confirmed with the client or specialist supplier.

Cooling

The temperature at which beer is kept and served is an important factor. The two are not always the same. Recent fashion has tended towards colder dispensing; the exception to this is what has become known as 'real ale'.

Cooling may be either:
- in cellar
- on cold shelves
- on pipeline. This will probably take the form of an under-counter cooling unit.

Specific requirements should be checked with:
- the supplier
- the client

Bars

Sizes of cast iron tables are fairly standard (eg Britannia tables), but other types are almost infinitely variable, **19**. Fixed seating can vary from practically minimum to opulently upholstered units, **20**. Stools are shown in **21**.

15 *Bar counter top:*

a *Plan, average centres of dispense points shown, sizes vary according to brand*

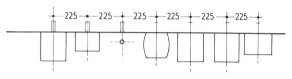

b *Elevation, heights also vary according to brand*

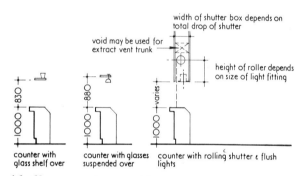

16 *Above counter canopies:*
a *Counter with glass shelf over*
b *Counter with glasses suspended over*
c *Counter with roller shutter and flush lights. Lockable roller shutter of this kind is essential where room in which the counter is situated is required for use outside licensed hours*

17 *Elevation to bar back fitting*

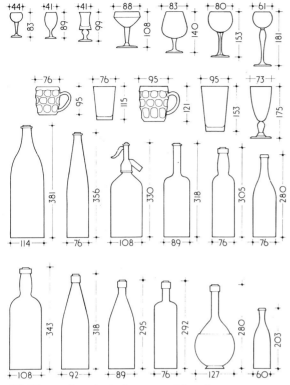

18 *Sizes of typical glasses and bottles*

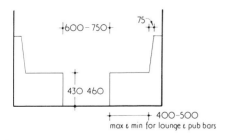

19 *Typical traditional cast iron pub tables, the round form is Britannia*

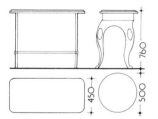

20 *Fixed seating of the bench type:*
a *Section through booth*

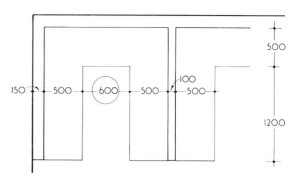

b *Typical plan of peninsular seating*

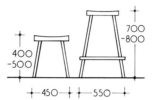

21 *Stools:*
a *Low stools for use at tables*
b *High stools for sitting at the bar*

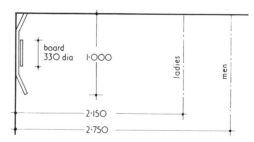

22 *Space required for darts*

Cill heights should be arranged with due regard for the fixed seating.

Ceiling heights are infinitely variable and depend on the type of pub and the required effect.

Space may be required in the various bars for the following:

- dartboard, **22**
- juke box, sizes vary considerably
- fruit machine, **23**
- piano or organ, **24**
- bar billiards and pool, **22** to **27**

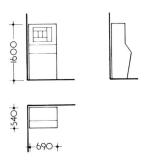

23 *Typical large fruit machine. Electricity supply required*

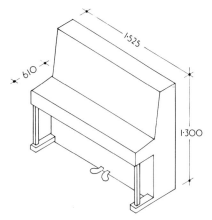

24 *Public house piano*

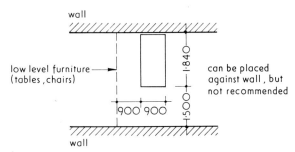

low level furniture (tables, chairs)

can be placed against wall, but not recommended

25 *Bar billiards with cue space (for short cues) at one end only, now being supplanted by pool*

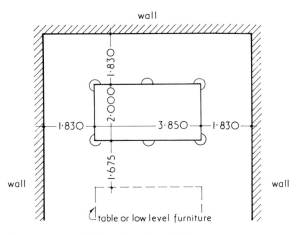

table or low level furniture

26 *Full-size billiards table with cue space round, now re-appearing in pubs on a very limited scale*

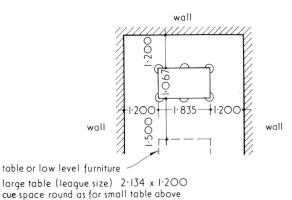

table or low level furniture

large table (league size) 2·134 x 1·200
cue space round as for small table above

27 *Smallest size of pool table with cue space (for short cues), now becoming very popular*

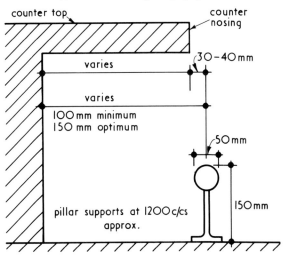

28 *Design of footrail*

Bibliography

This bibliography does not attempt to list the innumerable building studies of new public houses which have appeared regularly in *The Architects' Journal* and other magazines. Instead, it is confined to books and articles of historical and social interest, or to those dealing with the general principles of pub design.

Books

Burke, Thomas *English Inns* (Britain in Pictures Series) William Collins, London 1943.

Burke, Thomas *The English Inn* (English Heritage Series) Longman & Co., London 1930; illustrated edition 1931; revised with plates Herbert Jenkins, London 1947.

Burke, Thomas *The Winsome Wench. The Story of a London Inn 1825–1900* (Novel) G. Routledge & Sons, London 1938.

Burke, Thomas *Will Someone Lead Me To a Pub? Being a Note Upon Certain of the Taverns Old and New of London* illustrated by Frederick Carter, G. Routledge & Sons, London 1936.

Clarke, Thomas Ernest Bennett *What's Yours? A Student's Guide to Publand* illustrated by Robert Wykes, Peter Davies, London 1938.

Crawford, Alan and Thorne, Robert *Birmingham Pubs 1890–1939* Centre for Urban and Regional Studies, University of Birmingham 1975.

Day, James Wentworth *Inns of Sport* Whitbread & Co., London 1949.

Girouard, Mark *Victorian Pubs* Studio Vista, London 1975.

Gorham, Maurice Anthony Coneys *Back to the Local* illustrated by Edward Ardizzone, Percival Marshall, London 1949.

Gorham, Maurice Anthony Coneys *The Local* with lithographs by Edward Ardizzone, Cassell & Co., London 1939.

Gorham, Maurice Anthony Coneys & MacGregor Dunnett, Harding *Inside the Pub* The Architectural Press, London 1950.

Harrison, Brian *Drink and the Victorians: The Temperance Question in England 1815–72* Faber & Faber, London 1971.

147

Hogg, Garry Lester *The English Country Inn* B. T. Batsford, London 1974.

Jones, Vincent *East Anglian Pubs* with drawings by Leo Gibbons-Smith, B. T. Batsford, London 1965.

Maskell, Henry Parr *The Taverns of Old England* illustrated by Alan Gill, P. Allan & Co., London 1927.

Maskell, Henry Parr & Gregory, Edward W. *Old Country Inns . . . with illustrations by the Authors* Sir Isaac Pitman & Sons, London 1912.

Mass Observation *The Pub and the People. A Worktown Study* 1943; new edition Seven Dials Press, London 1970.

Monkton, H. A. *A History of the English Public House* Bodley Head, London 1969.

Oliver, Basil *The Renaissance of the English Public House* Faber & Faber, London 1947.

Piper, John *Buildings and Prospects* The Architectural Press, London 1948.

Richards, Timothy M. & Curl, James Stevens *City of London Pubs: A Practical and Historical Guide* David & Charles, Newton Abbot 1973.

Richardson, Albert Edward *The Old Inns of England . . . illustrated from drawings by Brian Cook and from photographs* B. T. Batsford, London 1934.

Richardson, Albert Edward & Eberlein, Harold Donaldson *The English Inn Past and Present: A Review of its History and Social Life* B. T. Batsford, London 1925.

Spiller, Brian *Victorian Public Houses* David & Charles, Newton Abbot 1972.

Wilson, George Bailey *Alcohol and the Nation. A Contribution to the Study of the Liquor Problem in the United Kingdom from 1800 to 1935.* Nicholson & Watson, London 1940.

Yorke, Francis W. B. *The Planning and Equipment of Public Houses* The Architectural Press, London 1949.

Articles

Bradbeer, Frank 'Public House Buildings: Design Guide and Technical Study' *The Architects' Journal* 29 March 1967, pp. 85–801; Information Sheet 1488. This article appears in a revised and updated form at the end of this book.

Curl, James Stevens 'The Vanished Gin Palaces' *Country Life* 22 June 1972, pp. 1598–1600.

Dunnett, Harding MacGregor 'Pub Exteriors: Case History of the Prince Albert at Golders Green' *The Architectural Review* February 1950, pp. 134–35.

Farleigh, J. 'Craftsmanship in the English Pub' *The Studio* December 1948, pp. 192–95.

Harper, C. G. 'New Ways with Old Inns' *The Architect* Vol. 101, 1919, pp. 107–9; 135–37.

Harrison, Brian 'Pubs' in Dyos, Harold James & Wolff, Michael (eds.) *The Victorian City: Images and Realities* Routledge & Kegan Paul, London 1973.

148

Hyne, H. R. and Musman, E. B., 'Pubs Today' *Architect and Building News* October 14 1959, pp. 298–312.

'Inn Signs at the Inn Crafts Exhibition Organised by the Central Institute of Art and Design' *Art and Industry* September 1948, pp. 110–11.

'Inside the Pub' *The Architectural Review* October 1949. Special issue devoted to the qualities of the English pub.

Musman, E. 'Public Houses: Design and Construction' *The Architects' Journal* 24 November 1938, pp. 822–23; 833–90. Speical issue.

'Modern Inns Issue' *The Builder* 15 October 1937.

Oliver, Basil 'English Inns' *RIBA Journal* Vol. 39, 14 May 1932, pp. 545–67.

Piper, John 'Fully Licensed: The Gin Palace' *The Architectural Review* March 1940, pp. 87–100.

'Public Houses, Inns and Taverns: Recent Developments' *Interior Design* January 1971, pp. 21–42.

'Pub Tradition Recaptured: Best Entries and Assessors' Report in The Architectural Review's Competition' *The Architectural Review* June 1950, pp. 383–96; 425–6.

Shipp, Horace 'In Praise of Beer Gardens' *Landscape and Garden* Autumn 1938, Vol. 5, No. 3 pp. 143–46.

Sugden, B. H. 'The British Pub: Its History, Current Developments and Future Trends' *Era* March/April 1972, No. 25, pp. 14–15.

Thorne, Robert 'Places of Refreshment in the Nineteenth-Century City' in King, Anthony D. (ed.) *Buildings and Society* Routledge & Kegan Paul Ltd, London 1980.

Thorne, Robert 'The Improved Public House' *The Architectural Review* Vol. CLIX, February 1976, pp. 107–11.

Wykeham, Hugh 'The Face of the Pub' *The Architectural Review* December 1958, pp. 366–73.

Index

153